Paths, Walkways & Garden Walls

A *Sunset* Outdoor Design & Build Guide

By Debra Prinzing and the Editors of *Sunset*

Sunset

©2011 by Time Home Entertainment Inc.
135 West 50th Street, New York, NY 10020

ISBN-13: 978-0-376-01434-4   ISBN-10: 0-376-01434-2
Library of Congress Control Number: 2011925915

First printing 2011. Printed in the United States of America.

OXMOOR HOUSE
VP, PUBLISHING DIRECTOR: Jim Childs
EDITORIAL DIRECTOR: Susan Payne Dobbs
CREATIVE DIRECTOR: Felicity Keane
BRAND MANAGER: Fonda Hitchcock
MANAGING EDITOR: Laurie S. Herr

SUNSET PUBLISHING
PRESIDENT: Barb Newton
VP, EDITOR-IN-CHIEF: Katie Tamony
CREATIVE DIRECTOR: Mia Daminato
ART DIRECTOR: James McCann

Outdoor Design & Build Guide: *Paths, Walkways & Garden Walls*
CONTRIBUTORS
AUTHOR: Debra Prinzing
MANAGING EDITOR: Bridget Biscotti Bradley
PHOTO EDITOR: Philippine Scali
PRODUCTION SPECIALIST: Linda M. Bouchard
PROOFREADER: John Edmonds
PROJECT EDITOR: Sarah H. Doss
INDEXER: Marjorie Joy
TECHNICAL ADVISER: Scott Gibson
SERIES DESIGN: Susan Scandrett

To order additional publications, call 1-800-765-6400
For more books to enrich your life, visit **oxmoorhouse.com**
Visit Sunset online at **sunset.com**
For the most comprehensive selection of Sunset books, visit **sunsetbooks.com**
For more exciting home and garden ideas, visit **myhomeideas.com**

IMPORTANT SAFETY WARNING—PLEASE READ

contents

Inspiration

page 4

Begin with our extensive garden tour and review the variety of design ideas for adding paths, walkways, and garden walls to your landscape.

How to Build

page 68

Here you'll discover extensive step-by-step instructions, drawings, and photographs that introduce a variety of garden projects.

Finishing the Look

page 136

You've selected the project to build and chosen the best materials and techniques to use. Before you get started on a path, walkway, or wall, refer to this chapter to review your design options.

Inspiration

Paths, walkways, and garden walls are the building blocks of a well-designed landscape. But don't consider them purely utilitarian or functional. While providing a way to safely and efficiently navigate the garden, paths and walkways can also be beautiful and complement your home's architecture as well as the surrounding vegetation. The material used and the linear or organic shapes created by paths and walkways speak volumes about your personal design style while also enhancing the outdoor environment. Low or high, made of stone, brick, wood, or concrete, a garden wall does double duty both as a divider of "rooms" and as a practical way to retain soil or to landscape with plants. Once you've decided where to place it, a wall becomes an important garden design tool. Walls bring a human scale to any outdoor living space and help define enclosures, gathering spots, and transition points. Add some plants into the nooks and crannies, and your functional wall becomes a living architectural feature. In this chapter, you will find countless ideas and inspiration for using paths, walkways, and walls as exterior design elements. You'll also learn from *Sunset's* landscaping experts, who share design tips and practical construction details.

Dwarf ferns, ground covers, and small perennials can be planted in just a few square inches of soil or in spaces between steppingstones. This narrow path looks verdant as it connects a stone retaining wall with the house.

naturalistic
paths

OPPOSITE PAGE: A layer of gravel, such as this blue-gray option, is ideal for a soft garden path. Here, the gravel connects a curved border to the right, a mixed planting bed to the left, and a seating area with a bench. It's an easy-care and permeable pathway.

RIGHT: An all-green garden is defined by a turf walkway that moves beneath a tree canopy and vine-clad arches. As the grass matures, it may become host to mosses, small perennials, and other volunteers, creating a lush ground-level tapestry.

Please do not gather the flowers

SUNSET GARDEN EDITOR
KATHLEEN NORRIS BRENZEL ON
aging your path naturally

>> Let naturalistic pathways follow the existing contours of your property. The curves and bends of the land, rockery, and native plantings will suggest the intrinsic beauty of a garden path that has been there forever.

ABOVE: Pathways of shredded bark or mulch are somewhat short-lived, requiring refreshing every year or so. But the cushioned surface makes for an inviting woodland-inspired walkway that's ideal for shade gardens and native landscapes. The material is often easy to obtain from local arborists or tree services.

OPPOSITE PAGE: Warm-hued native soil mixed with gravel creates a striking pathway and suitable growing medium for a coastal garden path that leads to a similarly colored stone patio. Grasses and perennials flourish along the margins of the path. The design allows seasonal rainfall to percolate gently into the groundwater rather than race into the street.

informal
paths

Informal paths often take their design cues from the natural walking patterns that have occurred over time. This soft woodland path emerges between the trunks of two trees, a barely suggested opening in an otherwise shaded area. There is no obvious edge to this path, which blends softly into the natural setting. Yet it provides a passageway for one to walk.

ABOVE: An orderly row of sunken steppingstones is informal in both placement and execution. There is a carefree balance between its straight line and obvious destination (the distant gate) and in the way it plays a secondary role to the abundance of perennials and grasses that tower above.

RIGHT: Irregularly placed flagstone creates a meandering walk, connecting several points along its course and ending at the garden plot. Its design is compatible with the rustic setting, historic architecture, and cottage-style herb garden. The sand-set stone creates pockets where lavender and other plants can self-sow.

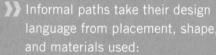

design lesson

» Informal paths take their design language from placement, shape, and materials used:

Placement: They are often situated in a secondary setting, such as a backyard or side garden.

Shape: They can take many forms, although often an informal path has organic outlines and a less distinctly symmetrical design.

Materials: By their very nature, materials such as gravel, mulch, or uncut stone lend an informal quality to a path.

ABOVE: The narrowness and the use of inexpensive gravel material create a casual, almost temporary pathway through a massive planting of annual nasturtiums. The simple design allows one to quickly move through the space, although there's always the possibility that as the plants' tendrils and leaves reach into the gravel, the journey will be slower.

OPPOSITE PAGE: Just because a walkway is symmetrical and leads to a destination does not mean it has to be formal. The casual feeling of this cobblestone path comes from its placement and the charming surprise as it gives way to the lawn before reaching the bench.

formal
paths

LEFT: Repeating the proportion of the front door and mimicking the architectural lines of the posts, this formal entry path directs visitors to the intended destination. The alternating square-and-rectangle stone pattern is echoed by the geometrically clipped box hedges. Yet those rigid lines are softened here by the planted borders of perennials.

TOP RIGHT: A contemporary interpretation of formal path design, this entry walk has strong symmetry and balanced proportions. Bright green grass accentuates the linear stone, while clumps of black mondo grass border the edges.

BOTTOM RIGHT: While the floor of this garden walk has a crazy-quilt feeling, its irregular pattern still feels formal, thanks to the stone curbing, clipped hedges, and urn at its terminus. These design elements work well together and give the path its eye-pleasing formality.

design lesson

》 As if wearing a well-pressed suit instead of a casual sweater, formal paths and walks give a garden a traditional, restrained appearance. Here are some features to consider:

Architecture: If your home's lines are symmetrical or formal, the walkway or path design should repeat that geometry.

Placement: A formal path is typically balanced with equal amounts of vegetation (planted borders or a lawn) on either side. Use the path to create a strong central axis to link the front door with the curb or to connect with a focal point through the opening in a clipped hedge.

Materials: Build your walkway from brick or cut stone. A mortared path often looks more formal than a sand-set walk. If you select gravel or crushed rock, use edging so that it looks finished.

ABOVE: This modern, arid setting is bisected by a double path of square steppingstones laid in mixed gravel. The lines here are formal, created by a strong central walk-way. Secondary side paths lead to the front door and other areas of the landscape.

OPPOSITE PAGE: Curved paths can also have a formal feeling, like this classic front walk created with repeating bands of bluestone across a lawn. Grass fills the area between each piece of cut stone, creating a rhythmic, linear pattern on the S-shaped walk.

LEFT: A curving path often follows a course around a special feature in the landscape, such as the pond seen here. The gentle shape and the use of crushed rock complement the informal setting of perennials, water, and lawn. As the path turns the bend, it meets a bench—an inviting destination.

TOP RIGHT: Together, circles and arcs form a playful pattern across the surface of this S-curved walkway. The positive-negative dot pattern is made with two shades of composite cast stone surrounded by a thin metal edging.

BOTTOM RIGHT: The arc of this path embraces an island of perennials, shrubs, and trees, while steppingstones set in the turf follow the outline of the garden bed. The path's various stone sizes create a sense of rhythm through the space.

LEFT: Large squares and rectangles of bluestone form light-toned bands that sandwich minuscule squares of basalt. The L-shaped path illustrates how contrasting shades and differently scaled pieces feel cohesive because of a repeated geometry.

ABOVE: Sometimes it makes sense to vary the width of a pathway. The narrower sections may encourage pedestrians to slow their journey, while the wider sections are obvious gathering points for more than one. Here, sand-colored steppingstones are expanded halfway along the path as a "foyer" in front of the entry gate.

This checkerboard pattern uses right angles to its advantage, transitioning from front yard to front door. The staggered rows of square concrete pavers add design interest and accommodate planting pockets at the edge of the lawn.

OPPOSITE PAGE: Foliage plants, pebbles, and water define an Asian-themed landscape. Rather than following a straight line, this path uses the traditional "broken" design by bending slightly.

RIGHT: Fine gravel and crushed rock are excellent surfaces for Asian-style paths, which traditionally use native stone as a key design element. Here, the gravel path unifies and connects the entry area with an interior courtyard.

SUNSET SENIOR GARDEN
EDITOR JULIE CHAI ON

creating an asian-inspired design

» Traditional Asian gardens take their cues from nature's elements: stone, water, and plants. Each of these features can be incorporated into your path design. As with Asian architecture, artwork, or flower arranging, the most appropriate designs use a degree of restraint with a limited palette of materials and colors. When in doubt, integrate evergreen foliage plants for year-round interest and select locally available materials that will look natural in your area.

ABOVE LEFT: An irregular paving of cut stones is knitted together with baby's tears *(Soleirolia soleirolii),* a low-growing ground cover. Evergreen ferns are tucked into spaces at the pathway's edge to reinforce this design theme.

ABOVE RIGHT: Staggered concrete pavers are surrounded by smooth pebble mulch. This permeable pathway accommodates plants that grow along its edges, while the pebbles ensure proper drainage during storms.

OPPOSITE PAGE: A simple combination of three elements creates an appealing Zen-style pathway. The compacted fine gravel walkway has zigzag granite block edging. Masses of Japanese forest grass *(Hakonechloa macra)* provide an organic counterpoint to the stone.

LEFT: A stylized picket fence with a swinging gate is the obvious garden entry. Two oversized urns, placed on either side of the cobblestone path, reinforce the sensation of entrance. Anytime you can mark either edge of an opening with a vertical element like a pair of containers or two pillars, the entry will have a heightened sense of drama.

ABOVE: This garden portal is accented with a single square steppingstone. Set into the gravel path, the stone serves as a threshold into the garden—just like a welcome mat.

TOP LEFT: The flagstone pathway that intersects this entry courtyard leads to the home's front door; its design is well integrated into the gravel on either side. The stone path accommodates the garden's high-traffic activities, while the gravel spaces are suitable for seating and planting beds.

BOTTOM LEFT: As the mortared flagstone path approaches the front of this house, it takes one step up to a covered seating area. The subtle grade change converts the path to a gathering place and seamlessly connects the indoor and outdoor living areas of this property. A low stone wall appears on either side of the step, partially enclosing the area. The wall accommodates containers and provides extra seating.

OPPOSITE PAGE: A simple, straight path, adorned on either side with exuberant cottage garden beds, connects public and private areas of this entry garden. While the crushed rock and the plantings are informal in design, the use of brick edging helps to contain both elements. Even the placement of two ball finials reinforces the feeling of entry and transition.

side garden
paths

Gaps between
steppingstones
become an instant
pocket garden
with annuals and
ground covers,
making a narrow
side garden more
inviting.

Getting from here to there could easily be a utilitarian endeavor with a ramrod-straight path. But here, off-the-shelf square stepping-stones are given a touch of style with alternating placement along the path. This is now a side garden that offers an enjoyable—and attractive—journey through softly planted borders.

SUNSET HEAD GARDENER
RICK LAFRENTZ ON
laying out a path

›› Create a cohesive journey for a steppingstone path by aligning each stone to an adjacent one. Line up straightedged stones with the edge of the next one. For curved and oddly shaped stones, follow the convex or concave arcs as if fitting puzzle pieces together.

ABOVE LEFT: As with the design challenges offered by an indoor hall, the walkways and paths that squeeze between your house and a neighbor's are usually viewed as hard-to-design spaces. But you can turn any passageway into a delightful garden journey with plants. Walls and fences to your right and left call out for a trellis that supports climbing plants such as these sweet peas. Pretty soon, the ugly will look unbelievable—and you'll forget how narrow the space really is.

ABOVE RIGHT: While this paved walkway runs along the entire length of the house to the left, it doesn't feel long or narrow because of the vine-clad arbor installed at the halfway point. The arbor creates a doorway-style opening with see-through trellising on either side, separating the path into two distinct spaces.

RIGHT: Irregular steppingstones are paired with sweet violet *(Viola odorata),* making a side path into an elegant garden feature. The self-sowing ground cover adds color, texture, and a light fragrance to the pathway.

A secret garden bench occupies the space between a side path and a lattice-work fence, turning a passageway into a serene outdoor room. With colorful cushions and a decorative urn, the diminutive space becomes a focal point to the path design.

OPPOSITE PAGE: Lawn and crushed rock define a garden pathway. The design is created with sunken metal rings. Sod has been replaced with a layer of crushed rock, which creates a beautiful series of steps to walk on.

TOP RIGHT: A spiral design turns this path into a work of garden art. View the labyrinth from afar or step onto the path for a meditative journey to the center. A circular ribbon of lawn forms the walking route, while smooth pebbles and ground covers add contrast.

BOTTOM RIGHT: In this herb garden, the path follows the circular raised beds. The gravel is easily contained by thin, curved wood edging, creating an attractive but low-maintenance garden floor.

TOP LEFT: A simple stone bench emerges from a narrow space between flagstone pavers, interrupting the path with an unexpected place to sit. Other spaces are planted with ground covers such as moss, thyme, and dymondia for an eye-pleasing design.

BOTTOM LEFT: The linear pattern in this stone path makes for an interesting design detail. While it divides raised planting areas, the path also provides an extraordinary, carpet-like surface in the cutting garden.

OPPOSITE PAGE: "Floating" pads of cut stone form the entry walk to this contemporary house. The otherwise linear pathway gains visual interest from the stone's offset and staggered spacing. The wall to the right doubles as a water feature.

transition paths

LEFT: Charcoal-colored stone pavers pair well with similarly colored smooth river rock to create a walkway that easily connects the home's foyer with a covered courtyard. The darker path offsets the architecture's warm wood surfaces.

OPPOSITE PAGE, TOP: A triangular sailcloth hung from the house, garage, and garden wall forms a "ceiling" that covers an interior garden room. Light-toned crushed rock covers the ground, connecting with a path that leads through the landscape.

OPPOSITE PAGE, BOTTOM: Poured concrete transitions between the court-yard and garden as it moves through an arched doorway to the garden. The con-crete is finished with sand-colored pigment and textured to echo the surface of the entry walls.

design lesson

>> The blending of interior and exterior design is more prevalent than ever, thanks to the wide selection of path and walkway materials that are also suitable for inside the home. Here are a few things to consider:

» The most important connection between inside and outside spaces occurs at the threshold of a doorway. This is where you'll need to address any grade changes, steps, or drainage issues.

» Poured concrete and mortared stone or brick are easy-to-clean surfaces that can be used equally well in a garden path or on the floor of a sunroom or covered patio.

» Reapply a sealant every year or so to protect stone and tile from the elements.

TOP LEFT: The refined style of this outdoor living area borrows the scale and finishes you might see indoors. The stone floor anchors this space, while a low wall encloses it.

TOP RIGHT: Paved in cut bluestone, a wrap-around walkway is the connection between this home's double French doors and the garden. Square columns support the covered arbor and create an outdoor hallway where additional seating or dining activities can occur.

BOTTOM LEFT: Fine gravel unifies every feature in this landscape, defining the floor of the covered dining area and moving through the rest of the garden as a pathway and planting medium.

A walled courtyard uses a floor of crushed rock and square steppingstones to link the interior of the house with the garden beyond. This private space has room-like proportions, which makes it a fitting transition to the outdoors.

around the pool

Honed pavers connect two distinct areas of the garden. The sand-set material forms a traditional poolside patio with furniture and an umbrella. In the adjacent walkway, the pavers are casually laid into a bed of tumbled river rock.

RIGHT: Wood decking and a stone patio are combined on either side of a reflection pool. Like a floating raft, the modular decking extends from the pavilion over the water's edge. In the foreground, wood slats are installed flush with the stone to create a walkway.

BELOW: Mortared bluestone laid in an ashlar design wraps around a swimming pool and has a seamless connection with the cast stone coping. The walkway leads to the far side of the garden, yet it is wide enough for a chaise, umbrella, or cafe set.

walls for
privacy

OPPOSITE PAGE: An ochre-tinted stuccoed wall is a sculptural garden accent that forms a semi-enclosed courtyard.

ABOVE: A stone-clad wall forms a U-shaped niche in an auto court. Yes, you can park an extra car here, but this is also a lovely focal point, with an attractive gravel floor pattern and groupings of large pottery. The walls are built from concrete block with a natural veneer of thin flagstones as the finished surface.

RIGHT: Adding a window cutout requires some skill; hire a licensed mason if you are concerned about attempting it yourself. The result is a wall that provides privacy but is also a charming place to train a climbing rose and capture glimpses of the garden beyond.

TOP LEFT: Two materials enclose this patio as privacy screening and a low retaining wall. Translucent panels are mounted between weathered steel posts to screen the seating area while also allowing light to pass into the space. The effect is modern and inviting, especially when the area is lit at dusk. The curved flagstone wall contains a large planting bed, provides additional seating, and extends to form a circular fire pit.

BOTTOM LEFT: This entry garden illustrates two wall treatments that work well together. The concrete block wall to the right is an affordable solution to a privacy wall. It is adjacent to a section of faux dry-stack stone that lends style to a concrete block bench. The evenly cut stone has the look of a dry-stacked wall, but it is supported by an inner core of concrete as a stabilizer.

OPPOSITE PAGE: Here, dual walls enclose a walk and contain plantings. The outer concrete wall, clad in a smooth, saffron-colored stucco, serves as both a privacy wall and a design element. In front, a wall of cut stone becomes a raised bed for ornamental grasses. Finished with a cap of flagstone, it can double as a garden bench.

LEFT: A low stacked-stone wall gives structure and definition to this hillside garden, fitting naturally into the setting. The stones are laid without mortar. The organic shapes of the stones are more suited to curved walls than straightedged cut stones would be.

ABOVE: A low stone wall is the perfect choice for a raised bed. The angular stones are carefully stacked without mortar, while other pavers are cut and mortared in place to create a ledge along the top.

RIGHT: Recycled concrete chunks are stacked alongside a grass-and-timber staircase to retain a hillside. As the concrete rows are stacked, each receives a layer of mortar to glue it into place. To accommodate a retaining wall of this height, the hillside needed to be partially excavated to stabilize and address drainage issues.

OPPOSITE PAGE, TOP: Finished with smooth stucco, a low concrete retaining wall spans this front yard, helping to create a level planting area. The stucco has been stained to match two brick planter boxes on either side of the staircase and to complement poured concrete used on the home's front porch.

OPPOSITE PAGE, BOTTOM: Annuals and perennials pop against a hot pink retaining wall. Built from concrete block, the zigzag wall is finished with smooth stucco and painted to become a garden focal point.

RIGHT: A low concrete retaining wall fulfills several design needs in this contemporary garden. It encloses the round patio, drawing attention to the central fire element. It contains plants in the adjacent planting bed. And topped with a band of wood, it becomes a bench for gathering.

accent walls

S-shaped detailing at the end of a low, freestanding wall gives a focal point to the garden. Made from stucco-covered concrete, the design is a foil for herbs, perennials, and a rustic urn placed in its curve.

TOP: An accent wall is the destination at the end of a flagstone path that meanders through a drought-tolerant garden. Slightly curved and made wide enough to serve as a bench, the freestanding stuccoed wall defines the edge of the garden while showcasing plants seen in the background.

BOTTOM: This dramatic curved red wall creates a color story and seating at the same time. The wall follows a curve while also forming a strong diagonal line. A cantilevered bench of shaped wood is affixed to the concrete, giving the appearance that it is floating.

ABOVE: Called a gabion wall, a term describing a wire grid framework that contains rocks or boulders and is often used to stabilize hillsides, this structure creates an attractive edge to a wood deck. The wood continues up and over the top of the wall to form a finished bench.

LEFT: Reclaimed logs are stacked similar to a tidy woodpile to create an interesting accent wall that shows off a cross section of each piece. The "window" is formed by a slice of metal pipe inserted while logs are piled up and around it. For this design to work, there needs to be a vertical fence post at either end of the wall.

RIGHT: Two freestanding walls in sunflower yellow make a big statement in this outdoor dining area. Built from concrete block that is anchored into the foundation, the walls are coated with stucco, painted, and dramatically up-lit.

terraced
walls

LEFT: A two-tiered wall terraces down a hillside. Hefty square and rectangular stones create a beautiful dry-stacked pattern that is complemented by plantings at both levels.

TOP RIGHT: A dry-stacked wall connects two garden staircases at its corner and serves as a terraced planter for ornamental grasses and perennials. The same stone is used as risers and step treads, integrating nicely with the mixed gravel paths.

BOTTOM RIGHT: Natural fieldstones were used to create a terraced hillside that also incorporates a staircase and waterfall. Because of the irregular shape of the stones, these walls need to have good batter, meaning they must lean back into the slope they retain.

TOP LEFT: Colorfully planted rows form a living wall that's terraced into a slender garden space. The composition creates an artful installation best appreciated from indoors.

BOTTOM LEFT: A stuccoed wall at the base supports a planted terrace. Levels are formed by lumber panels secured by metal bars sunk into the soil. The terraces are approximately 12 inches high and 12 inches deep, allowing for even distribution of soil weight on the hillside.

ABOVE: Sand-colored stone is mortared in place to create terracing that incorporates a patio, a pool, and a retaining wall. Natural stone is used around the patio and for the retaining wall. The same stone is cut into rectangular shapes that are smoother to the skin of bathers at the pool's edge.

SUNSET CONTRIBUTING EDITOR
PETER O. WHITELEY ON
building structural walls

›› Depending on the slope or grade change your design will address, a retaining or terraced wall's height should be considered. Check with local building codes to learn the maximum height allowed. In general, the height of the wall should be equal to the depth of the planting bed it retains.

decorative walls

A curved stuccoed wall animates this otherwise linear architecture and forms an inviting outdoor courtyard. The wall lines up with a small passageway at the edge of the garden.

ABOVE: Plum-colored paint turns two sections of a garden wall into a focal point. The walls curve slightly and are built of concrete block that has been finished with smooth stucco. They stand on either side of an informal staircase leading to the rest of the garden.

TOP RIGHT: The circular passageway in this mortared stone wall symbolizes a "moon gate" through which one can pass into the garden. The shape of the opening echoes the rounded water feature in the foreground.

BOTTOM RIGHT: A casually stacked wall of chalky gray stone connects a hillside with a gravel pathway. The builder has thoughtfully inserted a stone bench into the wall.

garden
rooms

LEFT: A cinnamon-colored stuccoed wall divides the outdoor living area from the rest of this property. The wall wraps around a wooden bench where friends and family can gather to warm themselves at the raised fire table.

RIGHT: A narrow side garden and an outdoor shower are turned into a garden room with the addition of a concrete bench at the base of the retaining wall. Upholstered cushions and colorful pillows add comfort, while a large framed mirror hangs overhead, reflecting light into the space.

BELOW: Terra-cotta stuccoed walls enclose the seating area in this entry garden. The color choice is a great foil for the planting scheme and is repeated in the furniture cushions.

walls for planting

A useful dry-stacked stone wall becomes a vertical herb garden thanks to the many planting pockets. While some plants may seed themselves naturally into the openings, these have been helped along by the hand of a gardener who placed rooted herbs and a little potting soil into the crevices.

TOP LEFT: An otherwise prosaic wall gains garden interest as a vertical canvas for flowering plants. You can create this look by training vines or securing the canes of climbing roses, as shown here, with obscure anchoring hardware.

BOTTOM LEFT: It's hard to tell where this planted flagstone path ends and the dry-stacked stone wall begins, thanks to all sorts of herbs, ornamental grasses, succulents, and annuals that have rooted in the nooks and crannies. Over time, a little grooming or weeding will be necessary, but for the most part, these plants look attractive even when confined to tiny planting niches.

TOP RIGHT: Artfully placed in an opening, the blue-green *Echeveria* is a subtle design detail. Succulents and ephiphytes (air plants) are good choices for wall crevices, as they require little or no soil and absorb moisture from the atmosphere.

LEFT: As chunks of mortar erode from this whitewashed stone wall, small planting areas are created for bromeliads and other tropicals. Similar plants grow in the recessed planting spaces along the top of the wall.

OPPOSITE PAGE: Stone planks form a rugged staircase that climbs up the surface of a stacked-stone retaining wall. Ferns, vines, and annuals embroider the vertical surfaces by taking root in gaps and openings.

How to Build

Inspired by the projects featured in chapter 1, by now you may be envisioning a graceful pathway threading through your landscape, leading to a restful garden bench or perhaps connecting your back porch with a vegetable patch. Or your imagination may be filled with visions of several attractive stone walls, softened by blooming shrubs and perennials.

It's time to turn those ideas into reality, pairing practical construction techniques with great materials—and a little sweat equity. Whether you're a beginner to DIY projects or have taken on many before, don't be afraid to ask an expert for advice—you can often find just the answer you need from local hardware or home improvement store staff members. In this chapter, you'll find basic instructions for a wide range of projects for paths, walkways, and walls. Gather your tools, plan your project, and dig in!

Where a thirsty lawn once was, an entry garden is now covered in permeable gravel with soft plantings and a prominent flagstone walkway.

evaluate the site

Before you begin any landscaping project, including the addition of paths and garden walls, assess the area on which you plan to build for a variety of factors that could have a major impact on how the job is approached. Knowing where buried power lines exist and whether or not a building permit is required will guide design decisions. Subtle changes to the curve of a path or the location of a wall can make your project easier and save costs.

PLAN AND ASSESS Follow this checklist for a smooth project.

» **Locate** property lines to be sure your project doesn't cross into a neighbor's yard.

» **Check** with your local municipality regarding zoning restrictions and setbacks, as well as right-of-way, height, and permit requirements.

» **Contact** local utilities to determine the location of buried water, gas, sewer, or electric lines.

» **Identify** soil type. The co-operative extension office in your community often provides soil evaluation for a small fee. You can also find soil sample kits at home improvement centers. If your soil is light and sandy, water will drain away faster and it may be easier to dry-set stones or bricks. Heavier clay soil drains slowly and will need more thorough preparation (such as a sublevel of sand and gravel) before paths or walls are installed.

» **Note** the topography. Slopes drain more quickly, and water may pool in low spots. A path leading up or down hills may require steps, or you may include gentle curves around a rise so that steps are not needed. A steep slope may be broken up with a retaining wall that divides it into terraces.

» **Identify** existing plants you want to keep. They may need protection, or they may need to be moved to a temporary "nursery" during construction. If a tree or shrub requires relocation, do this early in the process so you can get a feeling for the space without it.

» **Plan** for access. Large projects may require a clear route to the street for deliveries of stone or a spot to unload gravel or soil. If you are unable to use a driveway as a staging area, lay boards or a tarp over a grassy area to protect it during construction.

» **Think** resourcefully about excavation and demolition. Rather than sending excess soil or demolished sections of concrete to the landfill, be inventive about keeping that material on the property. When digging a foundation for a path, for instance, consider building low mounds on either side. Repurposed concrete pieces can be stacked to create raised planting beds in a vegetable garden.

» **Draw** a plan for how your project will fit into the existing landscape. This can be a simple sketch or a more detailed plan drawn to scale. Design trick: enlarge photographs of your yard and sketch new design features on an overlay of tracing paper.

ABOVE: The placement of this 20-inch-high stone-faced seat wall was determined in part by the roots of the mature sycamore tree. Warm-toned gravel allows drainage and is compatible with the rustic setting.

SUNSET HEAD GARDENER RICK LAFRENTZ ON
doing the math

》 A variety of factors may determine your project budget, among them the cost of permits, charges for the removal of existing landscaping materials, equipment rentals, tool purchases, and contractor fees. Do your best to estimate the cost of your building materials. Wall stone is usually priced by weight; base rock, sand, and gravel are sold by the cubic foot; and flagstone and cut stone are sold by the square foot. Solid or three-hole bricks are generally sold by the piece; concrete bricks are sold by the square foot. Visit a local stone yard or building materials supplier to get an idea of the costs for various materials. Locally quarried or manufactured ingredients are generally less expensive than exotic or specialty stone. Remember to factor delivery charges into your budget.

understand microclimates

Situated so it receives equal parts sun and shade during the day, this broad flagstone path winds gracefully through the trees. It's dry-set on a bed of sand and gravel, so rainwater soaks through the gaps between the stones.

Before you start laying out your path or wall project, consider the amount of sunlight and wind the area receives throughout the year so that your design works with nature instead of fighting against it. You may find that by installing the hardscaping a few feet away from where you originally planned means that the surrounding landscape will have a better chance at survival, wind will be tamed, and seating areas will be comfortable during the part of the day you plan to use them.

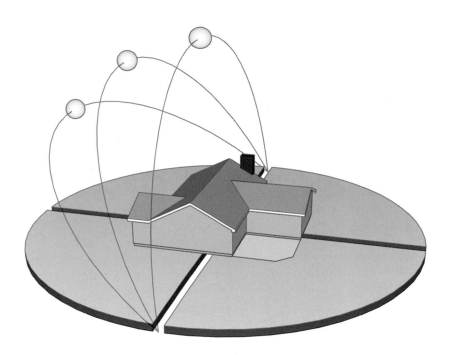

Track the Sun

Calculate how much time each segment of the garden is exposed to the sun to determine your potential enjoyment of the space. When you track the sun's course as it moves overhead, you can adjust the location, orientation, size, and shape of your path, walkway, or walls—and potentially add weeks or possibly months of sun or shade each year.

All other factors being equal, a path or wall situated on the north side of your home will receive less sunlight than one on the south-facing side. East-facing projects are relatively cool because they receive only morning sun. A walk or wall on the west side receives sunlight in the afternoon, which could make it a very warm space. In a hot region, you probably want to orient such projects on the east- and north-facing sides, while in a cooler climate, south and west orientations may be preferable.

Also consider the sun's path during the year (see illustration above). The sun's arc is higher in summer and lower in winter, which will alter how light and shadows are cast over each garden area.

Taming the Wind

Observe the wind's course and how it typically moves through your lot. Ideally, you want a gentle breeze blowing during the hottest times. Wind flows like water, spilling over obstacles, breaking into currents, eddying and swirling.

A solid garden wall will protect small areas from wind—roughly the same dimensions as the wall's height and width. Farther away, wind will swirl downward onto the garden floor. A barrier with openings, such as several short walls with gaps or alternating with hedging, will diffuse rather than block the wind and provide protection for a larger area.

More About Microclimates

Nearby buildings, trees, shrubs, and overhead structures create microclimates, so conditions in your garden may differ significantly from those on a neighboring property or even on another part of your own property.

Certain materials reflect sun and heat better than others. Light-colored paving and walls diffuse or spread sun and heat, but they can be uncomfortably bright. Beige pavers and siding are usually cooler.

accommodate for grade

A flagstone path with three steps bisects a low retaining wall. Together, these design elements help to transform a sloped area into two useful levels.

Not every property is perfectly flat. If your lot is on a steep incline or hillside, you may need to grade or level it to create plantable sections. Installing retaining walls or terracing is a useful and attractive solution to address sloped garden areas, make them easier to maintain, and reduce storm water runoff.

Hillsides that are zoned as "critical slope areas" or have erosion concerns require that you consult an expert professional landscaper or contractor for advice.

For gently sloped areas of the yard, suitable design solutions include adding low retaining walls or multi-tiered terracing. Here are some steps to consider.

GRADING AND LEVELING Improve a sloped area with garden walls or a few steps.

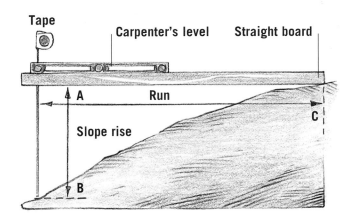

Assess the Slope

Determine the location of a possible terrace or decide whether the addition of one or two steps will improve navigation on a steep pathway. You can use a straight board and a tape measure to calculate the grade change. Place the board at the highest location, extend it out toward the lowest point of the slope, and extend the tape measure to the ground (shown at left). Make sure the board is level. Measure the overall rise and run of the slope. For example, you may find that a slope is 8 feet long (the run) and has a 4-foot difference between the highest and lowest points (the rise). These calculations call for four 12-inch-high retaining walls—one every 2 feet along the run of the slope. Gradual grade changes are more natural in appearance than steep ones.

Check Local Codes

Because of concerns about safety and erosion, local building codes may be in effect. In some municipalities, permits are required for walls higher than 18 inches; in others, the code height may be 4 feet. Check and comply with local codes before embarking on your construction project. If you are dealing with unstable soil, drainage issues, or uneven or extremely steep land, consult an engineer before proceeding.

Faced with buff-colored Arizona stone, the low concrete retaining wall shown above, which doubles as a raised bed and bonus seating, did not require a permit to construct.

Select Materials

The choices of durable wall and step materials are as varied as your garden style. In general, look for regional stone or locally manufactured brick or concrete block rather than exotic materials. Sources close to home will complement your landscape and will likely be less costly, since they haven't been shipped long distances to the stone yard or home improvement center. Select material that is compatible with your home's architectural style and with other features of your landscape. The scale of the project may also determine your materials choice. For example, dry-stacked stone walls become less stable the higher they are built, so you may opt instead for cut stone that will be mortared in place.

design lesson

» When you're designing a wall or steps for a slope, it is best to adhere to the natural contours of the property rather than carving extreme angles into the hillside. Terraces do not have to be 100 percent flat for successful planting. In fact, a gentle grade change ensures better drainage (see next page for more on drainage).

» Do not change the grade around the base of any existing trees. Retaining walls should not be built next to or around the root zone or flare of a trunk.

» While addressing grading issues, note how your property relates to your home's foundation. Areas that touch the foundation (such as a patio, path, or planting bed) should slope away from the house at a rate of between $\frac{1}{8}$ and $\frac{1}{4}$ inch per running foot.

provide drainage

Terraced stone levels follow the natural contours of this hillside garden. Stone paths lead to a bluff that's supported by large boulders and planted with ground covers that help contain the slope. Gravel flooring ensures good drainage as well.

By its very nature, any garden construction project will disrupt the native soil and affect how water drains through the area. Water is likely to run off even the most permeable of paved surfaces during prolonged rainfall or seasonal storms. When you install a large, solid object, such as a concrete retaining wall or raised stone bed, the natural drainage of the site is also changed.

Unless the site slopes naturally, you will need to grade before installing a path or wall so that runoff won't collect where it can cause problems—such as against a house foundation. In fact, accommodating for drainage should be the very first step in construction. Pay particular attention to drainage needs for large areas with impermeable paving, such as a concrete path. Gravel paths and sand-set stone paths probably won't need as much attention. Drainage should also be incorporated into any retaining wall to reduce pooling of water that will weaken the construction.

MANAGE WATER FLOW Smart solutions for controlling and directing water.

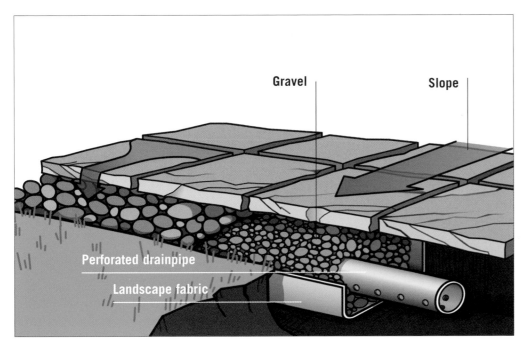

Gravel   Slope

Perforated drainpipe

Landscape fabric

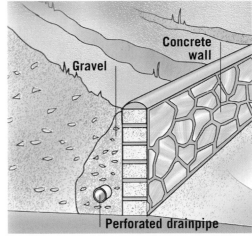

Gravel   Concrete wall

Perforated drainpipe

If you are planning extensive pathways or have poorly draining soil, you may need to provide an easy way for water to flow safely away. Dig a trench about 12 inches deep (deeper in areas where the ground freezes) on the downward edge of the path and line it with landscape fabric. Then add perforated pipe, with the holes pointed down so gravel won't plug them. If your property slopes, extend the trench and add unperforated pipe to carry the

water downhill to a point where it can flow out and not be a problem. If your land is flat, extend the pipe instead to a gravel-filled pit away from all structures.

Before you cover up the pipe, check with a level to make sure all sections slant downhill. Then cover the pipe loosely with additional landscape fabric and fill around the perforated sections with round, washed gravel. Cover solid sections of pipe with soil.

During a storm, plenty of water can seep into the soil and move toward a retaining wall. If the wall is built with dry-stacked stones or pavers, the water can simply seep through the joints. But if the wall is built of mortared stone, brick, or other solid materials, a great deal of water pressure could build up, which could cause buckling or cracking.

One solution, as shown in the illustration above, is to run a sloped drainpipe along the wall so it can carry water to another location. On a long wall, you may want to start in the middle and slope the pipe in both directions. Dig a trench during construction, situating it behind the wall. Fill the trench with several inches of rounded gravel, and lay the pipe on top. Make sure the pipe slopes at a rate of between ⅛ and ¼ inch or more per foot. Cover it with more gravel, top it with landscaping fabric, and cover it with soil.

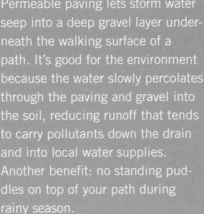

design lesson

Permeable paving lets storm water seep into a deep gravel layer underneath the walking surface of a path. It's good for the environment because the water slowly percolates through the paving and gravel into the soil, reducing runoff that tends to carry pollutants down the drain and into local water supplies. Another benefit: no standing puddles on top of your path during rainy season.

excavate

Many landscape design projects require excavation to ensure that paths are level with the rest of the garden and that retaining walls stand solidly and evenly in place. Excavation may also be needed if you are laying a foundation or installing drainage materials. A simple way to excavate to the correct depth across a wide area is to lay out twine between stakes and take your measurements from the twine as you dig. Any adjustments for grading can be incorporated during this process. The following directions are useful for prepping paths, patios, or terraces.

This casual design creates the comfortable illusion that cobblestones have sunk into the path with time. In fact, a few inches of soil was removed before installation. Any leftover soil was used to fill planting areas on either side of the path.

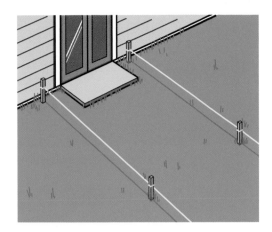

❶ Stake the Perimeter

Use stakes and string to mark the area you need to excavate. Keep the stakes back a bit, as shown, so they aren't in your way as you dig and build the path. If you intend for your path to be perfectly symmetrical, take measurements along the design at several points. See pages 86–87 for more details.

❷ Mark the Height

Establish the eventual height of the path by marking the height on one stake and tying a string to that spot. Then stretch the string to the opposite stake and tie a knot. Slip on a line level (a small tool that hooks over the string) and raise or lower the second knot until the string is level. Mark the height and repeat the process until you've marked all stakes. For rough flagstones that vary in thickness, use string lines to roughly gauge the depth of the excavation at the same time that you mark the perimeter.

design lesson

>> To mark gentle, freeform curves, lay one or more garden hoses on the ground in the shape you desire. Pour sand over the hose along its length. When you pick up the hose, the outline will remain. Before you settle on the shape, test any edging material you plan to use, making sure it is flexible enough to bend into the curve you want. Where precision is not needed, simply mark the ground with spray paint and cut the soil or sod along the sprayed line.

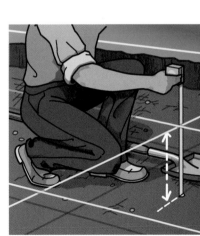

Level line

Slope line

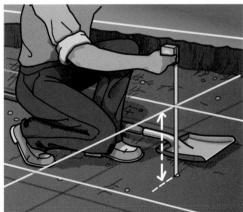

❸ Set the Slope

Paved paths must slope so rainwater can drain. Paths might need just ⅛ inch of slope per foot, along either their length or their width. For the gentlest slope, create a slight crown in the center of the path so water drains to both sides. To calculate how much slope you need, divide the distance of the path, in feet, by 8. The result is the number of inches the path must slope away from your home's foundation to ensure proper drainage of storm water.

❹ Remove Soil

Using these reference points, excavate soil. Dig first with a pointed shovel, then clean up the bottom of the excavation with a flat shovel. Remove all organic material, including roots and stones. (If you encounter thick tree roots, ask an arborist whether you can sever them without endangering the health of the tree; you might need to reevaluate your path design accordingly.) If you accidentally loosen too much soil, remove it and replace it with gravel, which compacts better.

soil preparation

Excavation of a bleak front lawn was needed to prepare this small area for its makeover. A pleasing grid of several pathway materials—including gravel, groundcover plants, decking, and large concrete pads—now occupies the space.

Unless you are starting with a blank slate, such as with a just-built parcel where a contractor has left things bare, most path and walkway installation projects begin with the editing and removal of existing vegetation. Once you have determined where to install a new garden feature and assessed the type of soil on which it will be constructed, you are ready to do the prep work. This can include removal of excess soil, sod, concrete, or plants. Before you begin digging, contact local utility companies to determine the location of any underground wires or pipes.

Sod Removal

The gravel base of a path or walkway needs to rest on level, undisturbed soil. To make sure you don't dig too far down, excavate in layers. Peeling off existing sod is step one. With hand tools or a machine called a sod cutter, you should be able to remove the grass and roots in a fairly uniform layer, without going into the soil underneath. Cut the sod into manageable pieces and roll them up as if they were carpet.

Concrete Demolition

An old concrete path that's basically stable can be stained, resurfaced with fresh concrete, or topped with brick, stone, or other paving materials. But if the concrete has cracked or shifted, or if it's not where you want it, it's time to grab a sledgehammer and demolish the slab. Many old walkways are only a few inches thick and relatively easy to break up. Others are thicker, with steel reinforcement, so they require more sweat. Gauge the difficulty by starting in an out-of-the-way corner. Protect your eyes, hands, and skin. Whack at the concrete with a sledgehammer. If the slab doesn't crack, remove its support underneath. Poke the tip of a rock bar (a thick steel bar about 6 feet long) under the concrete and tilt it up, using the rock bar as a level. When the slab lifts, push a rock underneath it to keep it elevated. Bang again with the sledge. Use lineman's pliers to cut any wire mesh reinforcement. For rebar, use bolt cutters or a hacksaw.

Soil Removal

If you have a large area of soil to remove or excavate, you may need to rent a front loader or a skid loader. Ask the rental company for detailed instructions on using the machine. Before you bring it onto your property, establish a route so the tracks will not damage your yard. You may want to make a temporary path with sheets of plywood. When excavating, position the loader's bucket fairly level so you do not dig too deep (be careful not to disturb nearby tree roots). Any soil you remove can be used to create mounds or berms elsewhere in the yard.

SUNSET HEAD GARDENER
RICK LAFRENTZ ON
laying foundations

❯❯ If you are planning on a path that requires mortaring to set stone, you will probably have to prepare a foundation, or subbase. Although it's heavy work moving and installing gravel and sand or concrete, don't skimp on the construction, or the paving may buckle and sink. For large areas, equip yourself with back-saving tools—a sturdy wheelbarrow is a must. Or consider having a contractor lay the foundation materials for you. The foundation needs to be deep if your soil is unstable—if it floods, for example, or heaves from frost. As you plan your project, bear in mind that small, thin paving units are more likely to be jostled by movement in the soil than large, thick slabs of stone.

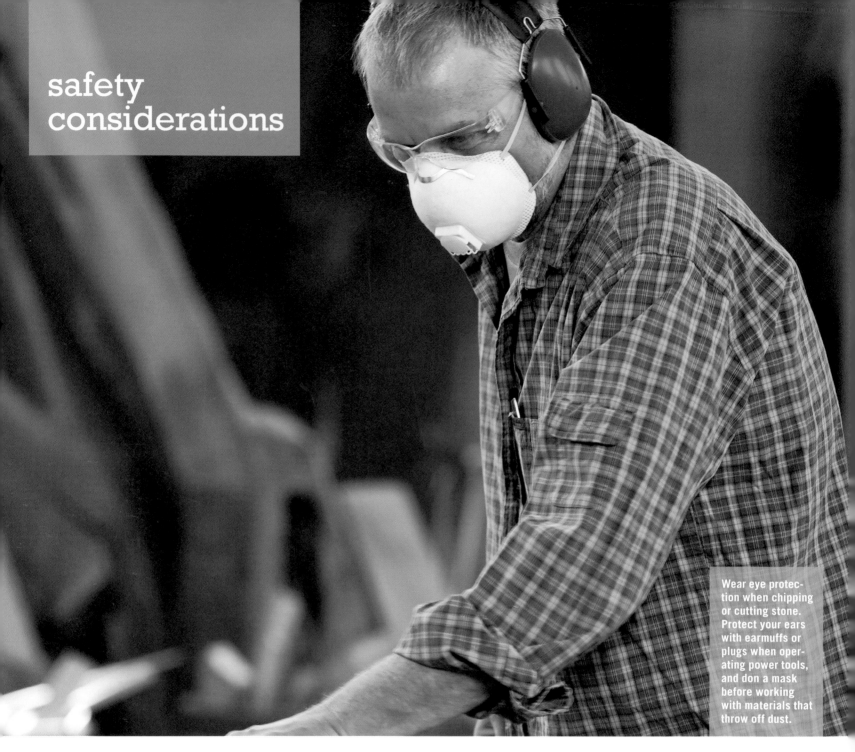

safety considerations

Wear eye protection when chipping or cutting stone. Protect your ears with earmuffs or plugs when operating power tools, and don a mask before working with materials that throw off dust.

Building garden paths, walkways, and walls is rewarding but also physically demanding work. Take precautions to avoid injury. Wear sturdy boots and gloves when you're transporting heavy materials, and keep out of the way of anything (such as a wheelbarrow or large rock) that might tip or cause you to stumble. On slopes, always start from the base and embed stones, bricks, or blocks firmly before moving up to the next layer. Start out with the right equipment for the task, and, if necessary, make it a team project, enlisting the help of friends.

Avoid potential safety hazards with a well-planned project that employs the techniques outlined in these pages. Consult your local building department about codes as necessary. Hire an engineer or landscape architect if your property has tricky slopes or poor drainage; they will be able to properly assess the work required to safely complete the project. As you plan, imagine how the finished landscape will be used, especially by children or other people needing a stable walking surface. Consider how the paths and walks may be navigated after dark. Think ahead and take into consideration any potential challenges before you start.

LIFT AND MOVE   Get the job done without injuries.

Lift with Your Legs

There is a reason some landscaping stones are called "two-man rocks." The construction trade uses this term to describe a stone that needs at least two people to move it. Avoid lifting heavy stones, pavers, or concrete blocks into position whenever possible so you lessen the stress on your back. Drag, roll, tip, or pry them instead. When you absolutely must lift, squat down and grab hold of the item; then, keeping your back straight and the item close to your body, lift with your legs. A lifting belt can help prevent strain.

Use a Ramp

To raise a large stone or paver into position without actually picking it up, make a simple 2-by-12 ramp with 2-by-2 crosspieces screwed to it every 16 inches or so. Carefully roll or tilt the material up the ramp. The crosspieces will keep it from sliding back.

Use a Hand Truck

To transport larger wall rocks or path pavers, or heavy bags of gravel and sand, a hand truck is highly recommended. A model with air-filled tires is easiest to push and less likely to damage a lawn. Work with a helper to load the material, then tilt the hand truck back until you feel no pressure on the handle. Use similar care when lowering the item into place.

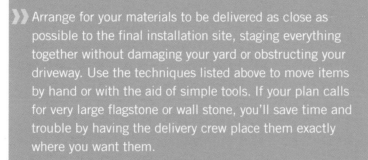

SUNSET HEAD GARDENER
RICK LAFRENTZ ON
having it delivered

>> Arrange for your materials to be delivered as close as possible to the final installation site, staging everything together without damaging your yard or obstructing your driveway. Use the techniques listed above to move items by hand or with the aid of simple tools. If your plan calls for very large flagstone or wall stone, you'll save time and trouble by having the delivery crew place them exactly where you want them.

your tools

The construction of paths, walkways, and walls requires the right tools to allow you to work with ease and reach a successful completion. Local hardware stores, nurseries, or home improvement centers will carry most of the tools you'll need for backyard landscaping projects. Look for harder-to-find tools in outlets that serve contractors, or inquire at a tool or equipment rental company.

LEVEL Used to check that a paving surface is flat or that a vertical wall face is plumb. A line level clips onto taut twine and tells you whether the twine is perfectly level.

MASON'S LINE Use with corner blocks to mark the perimeters of paths or walls to keep the paving edges straight. You can also use the twine as a guide for the height of a finished surface.

TAPE MEASURE Useful for laying out linear paths and walls. Choose a steel tape, 16 or 25 feet long and 1 inch wide (narrower tapes are more apt to twist or buckle).

GARDEN RAKE A metal rake with a bow frame will help you level soil, sand, or gravel.

SPADES AND SHOVELS For excavating, a round-pointed shovel is easiest to use, but switch to a straightedged spade to make the edges of a trench vertical and to square off the trench bottom. A shovel with a D-shaped handle works well for spreading sand and gravel.

TAMPER Using this heavy metal plate on a pole, you can compact a gravel or sand foundation firmly. Water-weighted rollers or rented power vibrators can also be used for these chores.

BRICK SET AND MASON'S HAMMER These tools are used to trim small amounts of material at the edges of a flagstone, brick, or concrete path.

EARMUFF HEARING PROTECTORS

SAFETY GOGGLES OR GLASSES

SAFETY MASK

LEATHER GLOVES

KNEE PROTECTORS

DUST MASK

STEEL-TOED BOOTS

HAND SLEDGE This heavy hammer is good for driving stakes and can double as a stone-trimming tool.

SPONGE A good sponge is useful for cleaning stones, concrete block, or bricks and wiping off the moisture before you set them in mortar. Tiler's sponges are the choice of many stonemasons.

RUBBER MALLET A few taps with a rubber mallet are frequently all you need to properly embed a stone or concrete paver or brick into a bed of sand or mortar.

WIRE BRUSH A wire brush is a good tool for cleanup. Use it about four hours after spreading the mortar to whisk away any loose crumbs and smooth the joints.

BRICK SPLITTER A brick splitter makes fairly accurate cuts without generating dust. Mark the cut line and align it with the splitter's blade or use the splitter's ruler to measure. Press the brick snugly against the guide and push down forcefully on the handle to make a clean cut.

PORTABLE SAW A circular saw or grinder with a diamond or masonry blade trims flagstone, concrete block, or bricks much faster than you can by hand. If you score to a depth of $\frac{3}{8}$ inch on each side, the stone usually snaps cleanly.

MASON'S TROWEL These are available in many sizes and various triangular shapes. Use a broad one for loading and spreading mortar and a narrow one for filling and finishing joints.

POINTING TROWEL There are a variety of tools, sometimes called jointers, designed for raking out and finishing mortared joints, but the tip of this trowel will work for most projects.

lay out and measure

Once you have determined the outline and placement of a path or wall, you will want to lay out and mark its perimeter. Some projects call for only casual marking, while others require more precision.

A linear path or wall can be laid out with batter boards. They are not easily bumped out of position, and they make it easy to remove and reattach the lines as needed.

ABOVE: This beautiful bluestone walkway follows a diagonal, stair-stepped outline. It was laid out with batter boards to mark and measure each corner before the area was excavated and the stone was installed.

① Build Batter Boards

For each batter board, cut two 2 x 2 stakes about 18 inches long. Cut a 1 x 4 board to 2 feet long to connect the stakes. Drive two screws into each joint. Drive two batter boards into the ground, about 2 feet beyond the corner of the path.

② Run the Lines

Take into account the thickness of any edging you will use. At the start of the path (for example, at the house, gate, or driveway), drive a single stake. Stretch lines low but not touching the ground between stakes and batter boards. Temporarily wrap lines around the batter boards so you can make adjustments.

③ Measure for Square

Mark the outermost corners of your path. Double-check for square by measuring diagonals, which should be equal lengths.

design lesson

A method called triangulation helps you accurately place a feature on a map of your property. Prepare a base map that's exactly to scale and shows at least two fixed spots, such as the corners of your house. Then measure from the two fixed points to another feature you want to map. Use a calculator or an online conversion tool to change both measurements to the scale of the drawing. For example, if the scale is 1 inch to 10 feet, divide one distance in feet by 10 to get the number of inches on the map. Set a compass to that distance and draw an arc. Repeat this for the other measurement. The intersection of the arcs marks the location of the feature, such as a tree, a piece of sculpture, or a free-standing accent wall.

cutting techniques

A flagstone pathway meanders under the canopy of blooming palo verde trees. Each organically shaped steppingstone was hand-cut to achieve relative uniformity with the next.

SAFE AND EFFICIENT STEPS Save time and money with careful planning.

Depending on the scope of your wall or path project, you will want to be economical when ordering materials. You can save money (and time) by designing paving or walls to minimize the number of bricks, stones, or blocks to be cut. If you need to trim only a few pieces, ask the stone yard or home center staff to make the cuts for you. They usually charge a nominal fee for this service. Or try using simple hand tools yourself (practice on scrap pieces first). Larger projects may require that you employ some of the tools and techniques used by professional contractors. Most of these tools can be rented by the hour or day. If you need to work over an extended period, you might save money by purchasing the tool. Be sure to wear eye protection anytime you cut or hammer stone.

Score and Break
A low-tech way to break or shape bricks or concrete blocks begins with marking the cut. Working on a flat, resilient surface, such as a bed of sand, use a brickset chisel on bricks and a cold chisel on blocks. Press the blade firmly into place and tap with a hammer to score a line. Score on all four sides of bricks and the top and bottom faces of blocks. Then hold the chisel against the score line, with its angled bevel side facing the waste side of the cut. Whack the chisel hard with a hammer, and the piece will break. Chip or scrape away any protrusions along the cut edge using a brick trowel or a brick hammer. You can also use a brick splitter (see page 85) to make fairly accurate cuts without generating too much dust or noise.

Hand-Cut Flagstone
Some types of flagstone can be cut easily by hand with just a tap or two, while others require stronger effort. Score a shallow groove across the stone by tapping with a hammer and cold chisel or a stone chaser chisel. It might be enough to score only the top, or you may need to score all four sides. Position the stone so the scored line rests over a scrap of wood or pipe. Using a small sledgehammer, hit the stone on the waste side to break it off.

Power Saw Use
The quickest, most foolproof way to cut bricks, stones, or concrete pavers is with a saw or grinder equipped with a diamond blade. Wear safety goggles. Use a tabletop wet saw (which keeps down dust and is much more pleasant than sawing dry) if you are working with bricks or other small pieces with flat sides. For a straight cut, place the brick or other material on the tray and hold it against the back guide, square to the blade. Turn on the saw and check that water flows to the blade. Slide the tray forward to slice through the piece. Making specialty cuts requires a little more skill. For angle cuts, use a special guide that holds the brick or block at a 45-degree angle or other specified angles. For cutouts, such as a notch, you need to make two short, right-angle cuts. Avoid overcutting by tilting the brick slightly as you move it into the blade. To nibble a curve, make multiple parallel cuts across the face of the brick by holding the piece firmly in both hands and tilting it up so cuts are slightly deeper on the bottom than on the top. Break out remaining material with a brickset chisel.

edging
details

Short wood rounds
line a charming
sand-laid stone
pathway. The
pieces of wood
create a playful
yet tidy edge
that outlines the
adjacent peren-
nial border.

Edging is more than a decorative band or trim around a paved path. In many cases, it keeps pieces from drifting apart and separates the path from the plantings on either side. If you're using large flagstones or 2-foot-square concrete or cut stone pavers, you don't need edging, as the pieces are heavy enough to stay put. However, a border will still enhance that type of design, as is seen at left. You can also skip edging where you are setting bricks or stones in a mortar bed. Edging is essential for sand-set brick, concrete pavers, or small pieces of stone—especially if you want to keep the pieces aligned.

Wood Edging

Wood edging is made from 2 x 4 or 2 x 6 boards that are straight and free of large knots. Use pressure-treated wood rated for ground contact or a plastic-wood composite. If possible, buy pieces in the correct length of each edge. Cut the boards and set them in place. Check guide strings and use a level to ensure the boards are at the correct height, either level or correctly sloped. You may need to shift gravel or tap a board down to adjust. Drive wood stakes about 1½ inches below the top of the edging, or trim with a handsaw (hammer against a wood scrap to prevent the stake from splitting). If the soil is hard, consider using metal stakes. To butt two pieces, nail or screw a splice about 2 feet long to the outside edges. Once aligned, work from inside the excavation and drive two 2½-inch deck screws into each stake. Shovel gravel under the edging to support it at all points. Backfill on the outside edges with soil and lightly tamp with a 2 x 4, taking care not to shift the wood edging.

Invisible Edging

Plastic and metal edging systems hold paving securely in place without drawing attention to them. Once backfilled, they can be completely hidden. Look for professional-grade edging available at masonry supply companies. This type is installed on top of the compacted gravel base, which must extend beyond the pavers by 6 to 8 inches, depending on the manufacturer's specifications. Plastic and metal edgings usually have an L shape when viewed from the end. Begin by setting a few pavers in place to define the edge, as shown at left. Then snug the vertical part to the pavers and anchor the bottom portion by driving spikes of the recommended length (8 to 12 inches) through the perforations. Stakes can be at 12-inch intervals on a straight run. They should be installed at shorter intervals or in every available hole on curved paths or if the ground is soft.

Curved Wood Edging

Form curved wood edging from redwood benderboard (about ⅜ inch thick) or from thin composite lumber, typically made from plastic and wood fibers. If the curved edging connects with straight edging made of 2 x 4s or 2 x 6s, use several layers of material that bends so that you maintain a consistent thickness at the top edge. Because measuring curve lengths is tricky, it's easiest to install pieces that are longer than you need and cut them to length once in place. Bend the boards into position at the beginning and end of the run. Temporary stakes can be added to hold them in place. Use a level to check that the edging is at the correct height or slope. Drive a permanent stake every 2 feet on the outside so that its top is 1½ inches below the top of the edging. Drill pilot holes and drive deck screws to attach the benderboard to the permanent stakes (remove temporary stakes).

Timber Edging

Pressure-treated 4 x 4, 4 x 6, or 6 x 6 lumber rated for ground contact creates sturdy edging and weathers to an attractive silver-gray in a year or two. Select timbers that are straight, as there is no way to unbend them. Excavate deep enough to accommodate several inches of gravel under the timbers. Cut and position the timbers using a circular saw. Treat the cut ends with preservative to protect from rot and insect damage. Set timbers in a bed of gravel and check for the correct height and alignment. Anchor the timbers with ½-inch-diameter concrete reinforcement bar (rebar) or ½-inch-diameter galvanized pipe. Equip a drill with an extra-long spade bit with a diameter as wide as the anchors you will use. Drill centered holes every 2 feet or so. Pound each anchor down through the timber and into the ground using a sledgehammer. The top of the metal should be flush with the timber.

Upright Pavers

Upright bricks, cobblestones, or concrete pavers make attractive edging. When they are installed upright, the design is called "soldier" style. Upright paver edging can be installed before or after you put in the gravel base. No stakes hold this type of edging in place. Ease of installation depends on having undisturbed soil on the outer edge. If your soil is sandy or soft, you may need to install paver-on-concrete edging or set the edging in several inches of mortar to secure it. Here are the steps:

1. Stretch a guide string to mark the path and make sure it is level. Dig a trench 4 inches deeper than the paver height. Shovel in 3 inches of gravel and tamp it firm. Pour about 1 inch of damp sand over the gravel. Scrape across the sand with a screed guide or straight board. Then spray the sand with a fine mist of water, add a little more sand, and screed again.

2. Position each paver so its outside corner is about ⅛ inch inside the guideline. After you have installed 4 feet or so of edging, lay a straight board on top and tap it to achieve a smooth, even surface.

3. Use a 2 x 4 to gently tamp soil or gavel on the path side of the edging. If pieces go out of alignment, nudge them back toward the path side by tamping soil into the space between the sod and the pavers.

4. To turn a curve, install benderboard (see above left) as a guide. Joints between the bricks or other material will be wider on the outside of the curve.

Tilted Brick Edging

This decorative edging adds charm to the path's perimeter. A design that orients the wide face of the brick toward the paving and tilts the pieces will be less stable than upright pavers, but there are a couple of ways to strengthen it. In areas where winters are mild, set the angled bricks in mortar, as shown. If you live in an area where winters freeze, pack mortar or concrete along the outside edge of the bricks instead so any cracks that develop as the soil freezes and thaws won't push the paving out of alignment. To install the edging, temporarily stake a wooden guide along the outer edge at the height you want for the tips, then check that it is level or correctly sloped. Dig a trench 4 inches deeper than the amount that the edging pieces will extend downward. Working in sections, 3 to 4 feet at a time, shovel a little mortar into the trench and place the bricks tilted at the desired angle.

Decorative Edging

Get creative with edging materials, such as salvaged building materials, glass slag, or interesting tree branches. If you choose a thin band of steel, it can be installed to contain a straight path or bent to outline a curved path. Depending upon the thickness and flexibility of the material, installation may be as simple as working with curved wood edging (see the instructions on page 92). Rather than using wood stakes to hold the edging into place, you will want to select metal stakes that can be hammered into the ground. Recycled materials, such as the stylish treatment of upended and partially submerged wine bottles shown above right, offer an affordable approach to path edging.

Brick Edging

Bricks can be installed end to end, as seen here, to create a finished edge for a concrete path.

design lesson

>> If you are installing paving that comes in set sizes, such as bricks or concrete pavers, you may be able to avoid cutting many pieces if you start with edging installed on only two adjoining sides. Place all pavers, then snug the final sections of edging up to the outermost pieces.

stepping-
stone paths

A steppingstone path is one of the easiest and least expensive options, requiring little time and equipment. The stones you select should complement the rest of the landscape; once installed, they will look natural and blend nicely into the surroundings. A general rule is that the larger the gaps between stones, the larger each steppingstone should be. For a natural look, place stones in a gentle zigzag that matches a person's gait. Stagger pieces so that one is slightly to the right of the path's center, followed by one slightly left of its center. As you work, walk across the stones you've placed to determine the comfortable location of each subsequent stone.

OPPOSITE PAGE:
This garden path promises a pleasant journey through lush plantings. The large flagstone slabs are placed intentionally off-center from each other so that people who walk here can observe details on either edge.

DESIGN ISSUES Plan for ease of use.

❶ Plan the Route
Lay out the steppingstones in a pleasing line, arranged so the spaces between them provide a comfortable, regular pace. Place them along the route so that their longest dimensions run across the path, not in line with it.

❷ Mark Positions
Cut around each stone with a spade or knife to mark its shape, then tip the stone on an edge and roll it to one side. Make note of its orientation so you can reposition it exactly when you are ready to place it.

❸ Excavate
Cut a hole for the stone with a straightedged spade. Slice the edges straight down, then remove soil or turf within the outline. For a path laid in soil, make the hole half as deep as the thickness of the stone, plus 1 inch; this will allow for sand beneath the stones.

❹ Lay a Sand Base
Spread 1 inch of sand in the hole and wet it with a fine spray of water. Tip the stone back into place in the hole and twist it into the sand until the stone is level and firm.

❺ Fill the Edges
Add more sand around the stone and pack the edges. Water with a fine spray, which helps settle the stone into place. Repeat these steps for the remaining stones.

SUNSET HEAD GARDENER RICK LAFRENTZ ON
designing a path

❯❯ Decide whether you want to set stones flush with the soil or elevate them an inch or two. For example, on a manicured lawn, you will want to set stones flush so that a lawn mower can run over them. But if the path traverses a soggy area, elevated stones stay cleaner-looking. If you plan on adding perimeter plantings or ground covers, research the mature habit and size of plants so that you select stones that won't be covered by the vegetation.

gravel
paths

Gravel is the easiest paving material to install. Crushed rock, gravel, and decomposed granite paths and walks present a casual, relaxed garden surface that's suitable for many situations. Because the loose material allows rainwater to percolate into the soil, it's ideal for areas close to established trees or raised planters. In general, gravel is best used on relatively flat stretches. If your path covers a sloped area, choose another paving or break up the route into flat terraces separated by steps. Gravel paths require regular maintenance, such as raking to keep the surface free of leaves and needles (or it can become a growing medium for weeds if the debris is left to decay).

Use the dimensions (multiply length by width by depth) of your path to determine the total volume of gravel for your project. Suppliers and stone yards are adept at calculating quantities if you provide the dimensions, so always ask for this help as a way to double-check your figures.

DESIGN ISSUES   Site evaluation for gravel projects.

Planted Paths
When what's required is only a narrow pass-through, such as access for maintaining garden beds or borders, a gravel path is an ideal solution. Here, it's okay that grasses, succulents, and perennials are creeping onto this little-used path.

Edged Paths
Gravel always plays nicely with other material, such as the stone blocks used to contain these raised planters. The stone creates a stable edging next to the loose gravel flooring and adds a formal touch to the design.

Sloping Paths
Irregularly shaped stones form the steps for each level of this path, while gravel is used on the flat areas between them. This gravel-and-stone treatment connects an upper and lower path with a consistent appearance.

SUNSET CONTRIBUTING EDITOR
PETER O. WHITELEY ON
improving gravel drainage

≫ A surface made with tiny stones, such as crushed rock or decomposed granite, can become surprisingly rigid once compacted, causing puddles to form in low spots. If you think this may occur, excavate about 8 inches deep and fill the bottom of the excavation with ¾-inch gravel that's free of fine particles. Place landscaping fabric over that area, then top it with the smaller gravel.

This generously scaled path has a center band of gravel bordered by 12-inch-wide stone pavers on either side. Both the gravel and stone edging are laid at the same grade, creating a visually seamless effect. This design application is an affordable alternative to a 100 percent stone-paved path, as gravel costs considerably less per square foot than cut stone.

INSTALLING A GRAVEL PATH Follow these easy steps.

❶ Cut Your Route

Mark the path outline, then excavate 6 to 8 inches down. Cut deeply enough along the sides of the path bed to allow the edging materials to be 1 to 1½ inches higher than the surrounding soil. If your path crosses a lawn, remove the sod with roots intact so it can be used elsewhere.

❷ Line the Bed

Install landscape fabric if you are using it. Cut it wide enough to extend under the edging and wrap up the outside almost to the soil line. Fabric pieces should be overlapped by 6 to 8 inches.

❸ Build an Edge

Install whatever edging you have chosen. See pages 90–93 for more about edgings. Be careful not to tear landscaping fabric if you are using it.

❹ Prepare a Base

Add a 3-inch base of crushed gravel. If the path area has poor drainage, use pieces with a diameter of ¾ inch; if drainage is good, the gravel size isn't critical.

❺ Add the Next Layer

Rake the gravel into a uniform layer, then dampen it. Use a fine spray of water to nudge tiny pieces of gravel into crevices between larger particles.

❻ Complete the Path

After any standing water has disappeared, pass over the area several times with a hand tamper to pack the gravel firmly. Add the remaining gravel, working in 3-inch layers at a time. Dampen and tamp each layer. You can skip the tamping on the final layer.

cut stone
on sand

Cut stone laid on a bed of sand makes a relatively sturdy path, provided the edgings are stable, the stone is laid in a tight pattern, and the joints are kept tightly packed with sand. Sand-bedding the stones provides a flexible surface that allows for easy repair should tree roots or frosts cause the underlying surface to buckle. Also, if an individual stone is damaged, it can be replaced easily if it has been laid in sand.

INSTALLING STONE ON SAND   Reliable techniques and tools.

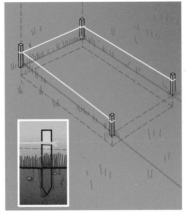

❶ Mark Your Site

Lay out the path's perimeter using stakes and string. When the stakes are in place, mark one at the eventual height of the paving, then measure up to a distance that clears the grass or other plantings. Make another mark there. With string and a line level, transfer this height to the other stakes. For drainage, allow for a slope of 1/8 to 1/4 inch per foot.

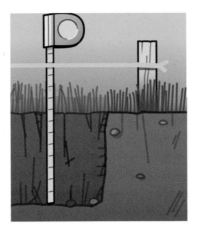

❷ Excavate

Dig a hole at least 7 inches deep where winters are mild or 12 inches deep where the ground freezes. If you are not using an edging or are using cut stone set vertically, excavate just to the edge of the path. If you are using metal or plastic edging pinned with stakes, excavate 8 inches beyond the path's perimeter.

❸ Build a Base

Install the gravel base and edging. If you will not be using an edging, install temporary 2 x 4 edge forms to contain the gravel. Add the gravel in increments 3 inches deep, dampening the material and compacting, before adding another layer. Build up the gravel until there's just enough room for the sand and stones.

❹ Top with Sand

Add the sand and roughly level it with a rake. Tamp it down. Take out high spots and fill low spots by running a screed along the edging or temporary edge forms. When the sand is level, compact it a final time and saturate it with a fine mist of water. Wait overnight for it to drain completely. Run the screed to level any uneven spots.

❺ Install the Stone

Aim to create equally sized joints, usually about 1/2 inch wide, but don't worry if you need to fudge by 1/8 inch or so to accommodate differences in the stones. Use a mallet to set each stone, then check its alignment with a level.

❻ Fill the Gaps

After you have set all the larger stones, cut and install partial pieces to complete the pattern. Fill the joints with sand. Do this by tossing the sand over the stones and sweeping it into the joints. Spray the path lightly with water and repeat until no more sand goes into the joints.

ABOVE: Tightly fitted square and rectangular pieces of smooth bluestone create a path to an outdoor seating area. Since this area receives a lot of foot traffic, this tailored path is an ideal solution.

flagstone on sand

Choose flagstones that are consistent in thickness, measuring between 12 and 36 inches long, and select as many straight-sided pieces as possible. A stone yard may allow you to hand-pick enough flagstones for a small path project, but for a surface larger than 100 square feet, you may need to purchase a full pallet of stone. Order stone at least 1½ inches thick.

If your site is poorly drained or if you live in an area where the ground freezes, excavate an additional 6 inches to accommodate a base layer of gravel topped with landscape cloth.

INSTALLING FLAGSTONE PATHS Steps to prepare and build.

❶ Sort the Stones

Stage materials, including stone, close to the project site. As you move the flagstone, separate pieces with long, straight edges so you can use them along the path edges. Store especially large slabs vertically, on edge, to reduce their chance of breaking. If the path starts at the house, begin by choosing a large flagstone with at least one straight edge for the spot nearest the doorway.

❷ Define, Measure, Excavate

Choose a level area and excavate, if necessary, following step 2 on page 101. Mark the edges of the path with string and stakes. Rake the soil smooth and tamp it to make it firm. If the depth is correct, spread 2 inches of base rock or crushed gravel over the soil. Tamp again, leveling the gravel.

❸ Spread Sand

Spread about 1 inch of sand over the path to accept the flagstone (don't tamp it down). The flagstone should be about ½ inch above ground level after it is set in place.

❹ Place the Stones

Set flagstone pieces on the sand, moving each around until you find a pleasing arrangement that requires minimal cutting. Place as many large stones as possible, then fill in with smaller pieces. Settle each stone in place by tapping it several times with a rubber mallet. Use a carpenter's level to check that the path is even. Add or remove sand as needed to adjust stones and retain correct height.

❺ Cut the Stones

Wearing goggles, use a chisel and mallet to break stones into smaller pieces. Place a stone atop a board, scrape a line on the stone where you want to cut it, then gently strike the chisel there to make a ⅛-inch-deep depression. Finally, pound the stone hard until it breaks.

❻ Fill In the Cracks

Pour sand or fine gravel over the flagstones and use a push broom to work the material into the joints. Sweep in several directions until all the voids are filled. Spray the sand with water to settle it, then apply more sand and sweep to fill the cracks. To finish and seat the stones evenly, set plywood over a section of paving. Run a plate compactor over the area; move wood and repeat.

pebble
mosaics

Light-colored ribbons of smooth pebbles paired with a background of darker pebbles are used here to install laid-in-place steps. This smaller project is a good one to try before tackling a larger pebble mosaic.

Using an age-old method of designing with stones, pebbles, and other media like tumbled glass or pottery pieces, the mosaic-patterned path can be an unusual, artful expression. Fun to make, this type of installation can also be relatively time-consuming. You might want to limit your first project to no more than 2 or 3 feet square, such as the mosaic stepping-stones shown here.

Draw a full-size pattern and gather enough ingredients to execute the design. Stones must be placed with their longest dimension upright, so you will use many more pieces than you might anticipate. As a setting medium in which to install the mosaic, use a mixture of 1 part portland cement, 2 parts 1/4-inch crushed gravel (with or without small particles), and 3 parts sand. You will use a slightly different mixture once the pebbles are installed. Depending on the type of edging you choose (see pages 90–93), install the path either before or after you have laid in the full gravel base.

INSTALLING WITH MIXED MATERIALS Get creative!

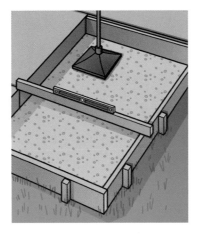

❶ Prepare the Bed
Mark the perimeter, then excavate to a depth of 7 inches where winters are mild or 12 inches where soil freezes. Install edging. Using 5⁄8-inch crushed gravel with finer particles included, spread a 3-inch base, spray it with water, then tamp. Repeat until there is enough space between the gravel and the top of the edging for the longest stones to stand upright with at least 1⁄2 inch to spare.

❷ Subdivide
If you're attempting a large mosaic, install dividers so that you can work in areas no larger than you can complete in a day. From 1⁄4-inch plywood, cut out patterns that match key elements of your design. You can set stones free-hand, but a repeating pattern will speed the work and produce more consistent results. Fill all but the top 3⁄4 inch within the form with the setting mixture.

❸ Place the Stones
Set the pattern, such as this diamond shape, onto the sand-cement mixture. Start by embedding pebbles around the pattern, laying them partway into the mixture. Pieces must touch each other and must have their longest dimension be vertical. When you wedge the final piece into place, the stones will become more stable.

❹ Finish a Section
Remove the wood divider and fill in the remaining area with a contrasting pebble color. Then place a straight board across the form and tap it down to seat the stones evenly. Repeat this across the entire mosaic (or the area you are completing that day).

❺ Fill the Joints
Wearing a dust mask, thoroughly mix 1 part portland cement, 2 parts 1⁄4-inch crushed gravel, and 3 parts fine sand (or use a bagged sand-cement mixture). Sprinkle the mixture over the mosaic and brush it into all crevices.

❻ Wet the Surface
Mist with water. Use a garden sprayer rather than a hose so you don't create puddles or wash away the sand. If holes appear, add more of the sand-cement mixture and mist again. Cover the area with plastic and anchor all edges. Spray periodically, keeping the area damp, for at least 4 days.

concrete basics

Many people use the terms "cement" and "concrete" interchangeably, but the two materials are not the same. Cement is just glue. Concrete is what you get by mixing cement with aggregate (usually gravel and sand) and enough water to produce a workable consistency. A basic recipe calls for 1 part cement, 2 parts pea gravel, 2 parts sand, and $\frac{1}{2}$ part water. Some mixes also incorporate fibers, acrylic fortifiers, and other additives.

The most common cement, known as portland cement, is usually gray. White cement is also available, although at a higher price. Pigments mixed with gray cement result in muted colors, while those mixed with white cement make brighter colors.

Known collectively as "aggregate," gravel and sand fill the spaces in concrete and give it most of its strength. A range of particle sizes works best because small pieces fit between big ones. The biggest particles should not exceed 20 percent of the thickness of the concrete or it may break apart. Use mason's sand or all-purpose sand, both of which contain sharp-edged particles in various sizes. Avoid play sand.

Concrete pads alternate with pebble strips in this modern and somewhat permeable installation.

INGREDIENTS AND VARIETIES   Determine the type and amount you need.

Cup Test

Check the consistency of your concrete with this simple method. Cut the bottom off of a plastic cup and set the cup upside down. Fill it with wet concrete and remove the cup by lifting straight up. If the concrete slumps to about three-fourths of its former height in the cup, as shown in the center above, the mix is right for pouring.

Squeeze Test

Properly mixed concrete is completely wet but not soupy. If you pick some up (wearing gloves) and squeeze it, the concrete should roughly hold its shape and liquid should not drip from your fingers.

SUNSET CONTRIBUTING EDITOR PETER O. WHITELEY ON

bagged mixes

» Labels on bagged concrete mixes can help point you to the right product for a specific job. The strength (shown as psi, or pounds per square inch) refers specifically to crush resistance, but you can use it as an overall indicator of durability and abrasion resistance. The higher the number, the better.

Sand mix contains no gravel, just portland cement and sand in a 1:3 ratio. Use for steppingstones or pavers 1½ to 2 inches thick.

Concrete resurfacing mix contains portland cement, fine sand, polymers, and other ingredients. Use it up to ½ inch thick as a layer over old concrete. The material is quite fluid, so you can spread it with a trowel, brush, or squeegee.

High-strength concrete mix is a basic combination of portland cement, sand, and gravel. Suitable for objects at least 2 inches thick, this material can be used for wall foundations, steps, or paths. It is relatively difficult to trowel to a smooth finish.

High-early-strength concrete mix contains a higher percentage of portland cement, plus sand, gravel, and additives. It's for the same type of projects as basic concrete mix, but the extra cement makes a smooth finish easier to create.

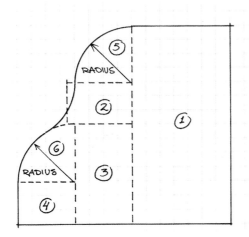

Calculate Quantity

Concrete is sold by volume. To calculate the amount you need, multiply the path's length times its width times its height. Measure the height in several spots to get a reliable average. If your path has curves or arcs, divide it into slabs or parts of cylinders and calculate the volume for each section. Treat curves as squat cylinders. Multiply the radius by itself, then by 3.14 (pi), and finally by the height.

design lesson

» Ice crystals occupy about 9 percent more space than the water that is in them. So when concrete absorbs water and then freezes, the ice can split the concrete. Here are steps you can take while working with wet concrete to reduce or eliminate freeze-related cracks:

» Add an air-entraining product. Available from concrete-supply companies, this material forms tiny bubbles that act as safety valves, giving ice crystals room to expand. Requires truck delivery or motorized mixing.

» Replace some of the mix with acrylic or latex fortifier.

» Barely dampen the concrete when you mix it. Pound the mixture into place.

» Use a bagged mix that contains waterproofing ingredients.

» Coat the cured concrete with a sealer.

Preventing Cracks

Small surface cracks are caused by excess water in the mix. These cracks don't develop into tripping hazards, but they are unsightly. Prevent them by limiting how much water you use and by adding thin fibers with other ingredients. Polypropylene fibers, the most common kind used in concrete, separate in a mixer into countless fine threads. A 1-pound bag is enough to prevent surface cracks in up to a full cubic yard of concrete.

Avoiding Shrinkage

Cracks caused by shrinkage stem from the fact that concrete slowly contracts as it loses water while drying. Long, skinny rectangles and interior corners on L-shaped walls are especially prone to cracking. Avoid problems by redesigning your project into squares and short rectangles, or cut grooves in the hardening concrete so that sections have stable shapes.

MIXING METHODS   Determine which approach is best for your project.

Truck Delivery

Save time and effort (not to mention cleanup hassle) with truck delivery. In order to avoid moving wet concrete in wheelbarrows, position the mixer's chute within reach of the project—usually no more than 18 feet. Standard revolving-barrel mixers may not deliver less than 1 cubic yard (that's enough concrete for a 4-inch-thick path approximately 4 feet wide by 10 feet long). Inquire about short-pour trucks, which carry ingredients in separate bins and mix them at the job site so you can order in smaller quantities.

Hand Mixing

Mixing from scratch saves money, although it can also be tough on your back. Bagged mixes need to be kept in a dry area but are fairly compact, while piles of aggregate ingredients can be left out in the weather but occupy a lot of space. Bagged mixes also help ensure consistency from batch to batch. Hand mixing requires only a hoe and a shovel, plus a wheelbarrow or mortar tray. Pour the dry ingredients into one end and the water into the other, then gradually work dry material into the moist area.

Paddle Mixers

This tool consists of an eggbeater-type wand powered by a heavy-duty drill, as shown. It offers the easiest way to prepare sand mixes and concrete resurfacing products. Pour most of the liquid into a bucket or tub with a capacity greater than the amount you are mixing. Add dry ingredients, then direct the paddle up and down in the mix. Rental companies offer powerful, dedicated paddle mixers. You can also fit a mixing paddle into a standard ½-inch drill for mixing small batches.

Portable Mixers

Rental companies offer a variety of portable mixers, which have a revolving drum and work well when gravel is among the ingredients (sand mixes tend to become plastered on the sides). Put in about three-fourths of the water first, along with liquid pigment if you are using it. Add gravel, then any dry pigment you are using, then sand, and finally cement. Mix after each addition. After you add the cement, squirt one burst of water into the mixer to reduce dust and prevent clumps. Tilt the tub back and forth periodically as the machine mixes. Add the final water in small amounts.

concrete walkways

Designing and installing concrete paths and walkways is a DIY challenge, but the payoff is a satisfying project that transforms the landscape with a clean, finished appearance. Concrete is versatile—it can be formed into many shapes, embellished with interesting textures, or tinted with decorative pigments. Before you begin a concrete project, read through these pages for information on choosing the correct recipe and determining unusual shapes and specialty finishes.

Enlist helpers and make sure they have the right work clothes and safety gear. Gather necessary tools, including anything you may need to rent. Your project will likely require at least one wheelbarrow, several shovels, a bull float, one or two magnesium or wood floats, a screed, a jointer, an edger, a broom, one or two kneeling boards, plastic sheeting, and a steel trowel.

GET IT RIGHT Match the correct type of concrete to the project.

Choosing a Recipe

Just as with pie crust recipes, there are many different formulas for concrete. But for projects like those shown here, two basic recipes work well. They differ primarily in the size of aggregate contained. Basic concrete mix contains gravel, so it's suitable for projects such as paths and wall foundations. It needs to be poured more than 2 inches thick. Use basic sand mix to make steppingstones 1½ to 2 inches thick or to resurface an old concrete path with a layer 1 to 2 inches thick. The layer can be as thin as ½ inch if you replace half of the water used with acrylic or latex fortifier.

Recipes and Ingredients

These recipes call for "parts" of various ingredients. Think of a part as a measuring cup that can change its size according to the scale of the project. Use a 5-gallon bucket as a convenient measure. When full, it holds ⅔ of a cubic foot.

Basic Concrete Mix
½ part cement
1 part pea gravel (⅜ inch or smaller)
1 part sand
Approximately ¼ part water

Basic Sand Mix
1 part cement
2 parts sand
Approximately ½ part water

Variations

Tweak the basic recipes as follows:

» Add ½ part more cement, plus a little additional water, to create a creamier cement. **Benefit:** produces a smoother finish with less effort.

» Replace up to half the water with acrylic or latex fortifier. **Benefit:** creates a denser concrete that's less porous and less likely to crack. For sand mix, this method allows you to apply a thinner application ½ to 1 inch thick.

» Add polypropylene fibers. **Benefit:** protects against surface cracks. For sand mix, this also adds stiffness.

» Replace part of cement (up to 15 percent) with fly ash or metakaolin and reduce the amount of water. **Benefit:** makes concrete denser, easier to shape, and less prone to surface cracks.

ABOVE: In a drought-tolerant landscape, poured-in-place concrete rounds of various sizes, surrounded by a base of Del Rio and Yosemite gravel, evoke lily pads floating on water. Patches of *Dymondia margaretae* soften their edges.

design lesson

» If you are embarking on your first concrete path, make the job easier with simple division. In other words, break the project into smaller sections and mix the concrete yourself. Build a grid or bands of permanent wood dividers from pressure-treated 2 x 4s rated for ground contact, or composite boards made of wood fiber and plastic. If sections are larger than 3 feet square, install interior 2 x 4 stakes, as shown. Drive 3-inch deck screws in partway to firmly anchor the concrete to the boards. Masking tape protects the wood from smears.

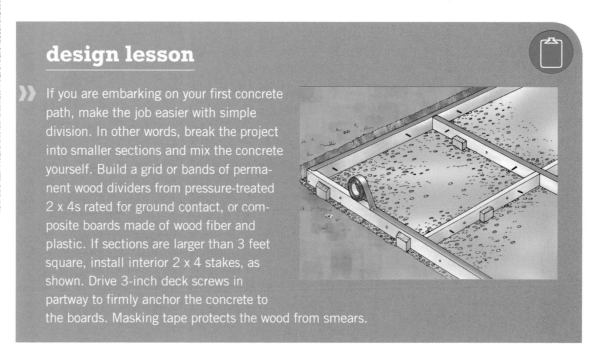

PATH CONSTRUCTION Work with a partner to make the project run smoothly.

❶ Prepare the Site and Build the Forms

Mark the general outline of the path and excavate at least 6 inches to allow a slightly elevated 4-inch-thick slab over a 4-inch-thick bed of gravel. Dig a few inches deeper if you live where soil freezes. Add the gravel base and then build the form (or reverse the steps, depending on the accessibility of the site). If you are using a vibrating plate compactor to tamp the gravel, install gravel first. If you are working by hand, you can build the form first. Build straight forms from 2 x 4s. For curved sections, use two layers of benderboard or a single layer of $\frac{7}{16}$-inch-thick composite siding (see page 92). Drive stakes no more than 3 feet apart along the outside and screw the edging to them. Slope the top at least $\frac{1}{8}$ inch per foot (or $\frac{1}{4}$ inch per foot if the path is next to a building).

❷ Mix the Concrete and Screed It Level

Prepare basic concrete mix (see page 111) or a bagged concrete mix rich in cement, such as high-early-strength (see page 107). Add pigment if you wish. As one person dumps the concrete into one end of the form and screeds (levels) it with a flat 2 x 4, another person should immediately begin mixing the next batch. Add each batch to the edge of concrete already poured, not in layers.

❸ Clean Up the Edges and Smooth the Surface

Run an edging tool along the perimeter to round over the edges. If rocks get in the way, seat them by pressing straight down with a margin trowel, as shown. Once water on the surface disappears, smooth the concrete with a wood or magnesium float. The surface should look uniform and fairly smooth. Remove the perimeter forms a day after you pour. Keep the concrete damp for at least three days while it cures.

Coloring Concrete

If you don't like the look of standard concrete, embellish it. Color can be added on the surface of freshly poured concrete before it sets, incorporated into the wet mix, or applied in a thin overlay on top of existing concrete.

Integral color Use a liquid or dry pigment for tinting bagged concrete mix. Or, for a wider range of colors, purchase dry pigment by the pound at a concrete-supply company. Take care to measure all ingredients—even water— precisely to attain consistent color. For the brightest results, use white cement rather than standard gray.

Pigment Color can be applied to the surface after you have leveled and bull-floated the concrete. Use a ready-made color hardener or prepare a homemade equivalent of dry pigment, cement, and fine sand in a 1:6:6 ratio.

Stains Acid stains react with ingredients in the hardened concrete and result in mottled color permanently bonded to the surface. The "acid" in the name refers to hydrochloric acid, which etches the surface so mineral salts in the formulas can react with hydrated lime in the concrete. Follow the manufacturer's safety instructions precisely. Water-based and solvent-based stains for concrete are also available.

Tooling Concrete

Easiest to apply on a path you can reach across, this decorative touch looks nice with tinted or stained concrete. Begin this technique after floating the surface with a bull float, edged the perimeter, and floated a second time with a magnesium float.

1. With a convex tool made for striking joints on a brick wall, press a design into the surface, pulling the tool toward you. For a flagstone look, distribute small and large shapes throughout the design.

2. Trowel over the pattern with a magnesium float or a steel trowel. Go over the surface to knock down most of the crumbs and any exposed gravel.

3. Brush the surface with a paintbrush or mason's brush to gently clear away remaining crumbs and to produce a finely textured broom finish over the entire surface. On a long path or hot day, skip this step; the concrete could harden too much before the entire surface is textured.

Stamping Concrete

Just like pressing a hand into damp concrete, you can add interesting designs to the surface of a path using templates and found objects. Texturing mats can be found at concrete-supply companies in a variety of designs. Use them to create seamless or repeated patterns emulating laid stone or brick. Or get creative with simple shapes, like the rim of a plastic drinking cup (see inset).

Before you pour the concrete, measure and mark the forms so you know the best place to begin stamping. After pouring, screed the concrete, float it with a bull float, edge the corners, and smooth the surface with a magnesium float. Then you're ready to stamp.

1. Apply the release agent. Follow the manufacturer's instructions on the label and make sure the entire surface is coated. Wear gloves as you work.

2. Position and stamp. Carefully align the first two or three mats so they are precisely positioned. Once you are sure of the alignment, walk on the mats and use a hand tamper to press them down. Work rapidly so that the concrete does not have time to harden (always have at least two mats in position so it is easy to butt new mats against them).

3. Pressure-wash and seal. Cover the finished area with plastic. After a day or two, spray the surface with a pressure washer, removing excess release agent to reveal darker and lighter texture lines. Replace the plastic and allow the concrete to cure for one more week. Once the surface is fully cured, apply sealer.

brick
paths

L ike cobblestones, cut stones, and concrete pavers, bricks are excellent for paths and walkways. As a uniform material, the standard brick shape is quite forgiving—you don't need to fuss about making each piece level, because that happens automatically when you finish the installation with a vibrating plate compactor. Preliminary steps include excavating, adding a gravel base, and tamping that firm, as shown on page 99.

Here's a twist on the traditional brick path. The sand-set installation and 90-degree herringbone pattern are conventional. But with the addition of a few curves, and the attractive border of edging bricks, the walkway feels updated.

CLASSIC OR CONTEMPORARY Brick and pavers are versatile for paths.

Choosing a Pattern

Bricks and other rectangular pavers can be arranged in numerous patterns. Many layouts eliminate the need to cut pieces. If you love the look of herringbone, you will need to rent a wet saw to make diagonal cuts. To make the patterns shown at right, the basic pavers need to be half as wide as they are long. Masonry supply companies have patterns that work with pavers of other sizes.

Pinwheel

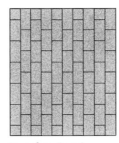
Running Bond

90-Degree Herringbone

Jack-on-Jack

Basket Weave with 2 x 4 Grid

Basket Weave

Half-Basket Weave

45-Degree Herringbone

SUNSET CONTRIBUTING EDITOR
PETER O. WHITELEY ON

concrete paver ensembles

❯❯ Many companies sell pavers in mixed pallets, which contain pieces in as many as six different sizes and shapes. These make complicated-looking patterns, but in reality the pieces can be assembled randomly. Sort the pavers first so that you can distribute the various sizes more or less equally for an overall variegated appearance.

INSTALLING BRICK   A great do-it-yourself project.

① Start Laying Pavers

This project shows how to install brick against solid edging, but you can use the same techniques with invisible edging or edging installed after the bricks are set. Start in one corner and set pavers so they abut the edging or adjoining bricks as called for in your pattern. A 90-degree herringbone pattern is shown here. Check the first few pieces to make sure the pavers are ⅛ to ¼ inch higher than you want (they will settle when tamped). If they are too low, make adjustments to the screed level. Set each paver straight down. Do not slide them.

② Progress Across the Paving

Periodically measure from a taut mason's line to make sure the paving stays in straight lines. Work on plywood to distribute your weight evenly. Leave gaps where you need to cut pieces to fill along an edge.

③ Minimize Cutting

You may be able to avoid cutting bricks at one edge. Install up to the end of your path, then move the edging to abut the brick pieces. With the pattern shown, some pavers still need to be cut, but only half as many.

④ Power Tamp

When all of the bricks are in place, run a vibrating plate compactor over the surface to seat the pieces in the bedding sand and force some of the sand into the bottom of the gaps between pieces. Go over the surface at least two times.

⑤ Add Sand

Scatter sand over the bricks and use a soft-bristled broom to sweep it into the joints. If the sand is wet, allow it to dry on the surface, then sweep again. Tamp the surface with the plate compactor. Repeat these steps until no more sand disappears into the joints.

SUNSET CONTRIB-
UTING EDITOR
PETER O. WHITELEY ON

choosing sand

≫ Work on a prepared site with bedding sand in place (see page 103). Bedding sand must be coarse, with a maximum particle size of ³⁄₁₆ inch, while joint sand works best if it is finer. Often sold as "concrete sand" or "underlayment sand," bedding sand can also work as joint sand, but you will have to sweep off particles too large to fit into the joints.

For joint sand, you have a choice between plain, fine-washed sand, or polymer-modified fine sand. The polymer type hardens once it settles into joints and is misted with water, resisting weed growth better than regular sand.

MORTARED BRICKS Start with a small path to get the hang of it.

❶ Prepare the Site

Install permanent edging or temporary 2 x 4 forms so you have a screed guide. The edging or forms should be higher than the slab by the thickness of a paver plus ½ inch. Make a screed out of a 2 x 4 and a piece of plywood (see page 101). The plywood should extend downward ¼ inch less than the thickness of the brick. Clean the surface of old concrete and coat it with bonding adhesive, or dampen new concrete. Prepare bagged mortar mix. The mortar should cling to a trowel. Working in an area about 5 feet square, shovel the mortar onto the slab and screed it.

❷ Set the Pavers

Dampen the pavers several hours before you start. Plan your design so that the top layer reflects any control joints in the underlying concrete. Using scraps of ⅜-inch plywood as spacers, set the pavers in the mortar. They will settle slightly as you install them. Lay a flat board on top and tap with a hammer to bed the pavers and produce a flat surface.

❸ Fill the Joints Using a Mortar Bag

The next day, fill a grout bag with the same type of mortar you used the day before. Squeeze the bag to squirt mortar into the joints. Keep folding the bag over as you work.

design lesson

❯❯ Use one of the three most common types of mortar: M, S, or N. M is the highest strength, S is the next, and N is of moderate strength, which is the best choice for most garden walls. For outdoor paths, S is best, though M and N also work.

❹ Tool the Joints

Once you have completed a 5-foot-square section, use a jointer to compress the mortar and smooth the joints. Tool the long joints first, then the short ones.

❺ Clean the Joints

When the mortar is fairly dry, brush it lightly with a mason's brush. Take care not to brush any wet mortar. Fill in any voids and holes with mortar, using the jointer to work it in. After several hours, clean the surface using a mason's brush and water. After a week or so, apply sealer to the entire surface.

wall considerations

Walls add a powerful sense of shelter and enclosure to the garden. They make large or open areas seem more intimate, and they give smaller gardens a sense of place. Walls can screen out street noise or block views from the outer world. Whether a wall is tall or short, its functionality and location can go a long way to improving its aesthetic appeal. Consider the wall a backdrop to create a pleasant contrast to foliage and flowers, making the plants look more lush. Brick, stone, and concrete are among the materials you will choose from as you design and construct. Placement, building techniques, and finishes reflect your garden's personality and style—and ensure your wall project will be successful and enjoyable.

Here, a low concrete retaining wall is finished with smooth stucco and topped with a wooden bench to create bonus seating near the patio.

WHAT, WHY, AND WHERE   Make walls work for you—and your garden.

What

Installing low, artful walls or sturdy, soil-retaining ones can add a lot of value to a garden. However, anytime you go "vertical" with a garden project rather than working at ground level, you need to pay special attention. Here are some questions to ask before you start:

» What wall style best complements your existing landscape, the architecture of your home, and the other hardscape elements, such as paths, walks, and arbors?

» What level of expertise do you have? If you are a beginner, start with a low, stacked wall that can create a simple planting bed or edge a border. If you have more skills, try a project involving multiple steps and materials, such as a mortared stone or brick wall.

» What resources do you need? Do you have access to the right supplies and tools? Do you have an extra set of hands to help, such as a friend or family member? Some steps are best done with two people, such as mixing and pouring concrete.

Why

A well-conceived wall can solve a design challenge, whether it's to divide a sloped area into terraces, create more space for growing plants, or provide enclosure or privacy. Think about the reasons you want or need a wall. And as you do, look for ways to simplify the process. For example, rather than building one 4-foot-high wall, can you break up the area with two 2-foot-high walls, which will be more stable? Can you use recycled material that doesn't have to be hauled to the landfill, such as broken concrete from an old driveway?

Where

Once you know the what's and why's of a wall project, the where should be evident. Garden walls can be divided into two broad categories: freestanding and retaining. Within each category, there are dry-stacked walls, whose parts are held in place with gravity alone, and mortared walls, which are glued together with a sand-and-cement mixture. Before you settle on a design, ask your local planning office whether you need a permit and, if so, what the requirements are.

design lesson

» Although retaining walls stay intact even if they have a gentle slope, designs that feature rectangular stones or blocks often look best when they stair-step down in level sections. Begin building such walls from the bottom of the slope. Excavate a level pad for each section. Then lay level courses on the lowest section until each course becomes the foundation layer for the next section. This will make the bottom stones appear to rise gradually from the ground.

stone walls

Retaining walls are common on hillside lots, where they hold back the slope or create terraces. They also have a role on flat lots. A low retaining wall filled in behind with soil becomes a raised planting bed. If you have a steep slope or an erosion problem, consult a landscape architect or soils engineer before you build. Many communities require a soils engineer to sign off on plans for retaining walls above a certain height—often 4 feet. Terraced walls and situations in which a driveway is above the wall also call for special review.

While subtle and not always evident to the eye, the face of a dry-stacked wall must batter, or lean back into the slope it retains (see illustration on page 123), and the top course must also slant slightly toward the slope.

EXCAVATING FOR A RETAINING WALL   Do the prep work first.

Step-by-Step Excavation

Before you begin building, you will need to excavate to create the rough shape you want. For a big job, consider bringing in a small earth-moving machine. There are three basic excavation strategies:

1. **Cut into the entire face of the hillside** at roughly the same angle as the wall will batter. This will mean hauling away plenty of soil (or moving it to another spot in the garden, such as for a mounded planting area).

2. **Build the retaining wall at the bottom of the slope** and then fill in behind it with gravel and soil. This also means hauling away excess soil.

3. **Using a combination of the first two steps** to keep hauling to a minimum, excavate the bottom half of the slope and use the excavated soil to fill in the upper half. As you excavate, be sure to leave room for drainage gravel if needed.

Improving Drainage

Water always moves downhill through the path of least resistance. To reduce the amount of water that will dribble through a retaining wall in wet weather, give it an easier route through perforated drainpipe. Create a depression several inches deep along the base of the wall to accommodate the pipe. Position it to slope downward toward where you want the water to empty (see pages 76–77). Fill around the pipe with gravel. If you are using landscaping cloth, drape it across the excavation and up the slope before you add the pipe, then fold the cloth over the top of the gravel.

design lesson

>> To reduce the chance of having mineral deposits (usually white) form on the face of the blocks, slip a sheet of building felt, also known as tar paper, behind the blocks before you backfill.

building with stone

Smooth, light-colored stones form this serene resting spot. Part bench, part retaining wall, the stones stay cool in the tree's shade.

Whether you're building a raised planting bed or a retaining wall, or terracing a slope, stone provides an excellent design option. As a do-it-yourselfer, you can reasonably construct a simple, 3-foot (or shorter) stone wall on a gentle slope with good, stable soil. Before you begin, check with the local building department to confirm whether you need a permit and soil analysis. For heavier-duty retaining walls, you may need professional assistance. Whenever possible, work with stone that is indigenous to your locale rather than something imported from far away. Your project will appear more natural and will feel established and connected to the rest of your garden.

① Set the Base Course

Once the wall site is excavated and prepared for drainage (see page 121), mark the approximate front face of the wall by driving stakes every few feet. Place the foundation stones in the shallow depression and align the front face with the line established by the stakes. Set stones so they nest well together. If you need to raise an edge, or even the level of a stone, fill in with gravel, not soil.

② Add Gravel

When all the foundation stones are in place, step back and check that the front creates a pleasing line. Make any adjustments, then fill in behind the stones with gravel. From the back, pack the gravel into crevices between the foundation stones and install a drainage pipe if needed (see page 121).

③ Add Layers

Continue adding gravel until it's level with the tops of the foundation stones. Then, starting at the ends or corners and working toward the middle, add a second course of stones, then a third. To keep pieces from wobbling, tap small stones as wedges into the wall from the front or the back. Fill in behind with gravel as you go.

④ Switch to Soil Fill

As you near the top of the wall, stop adding gravel backfill. Tuck landscaping cloth, if you are using it, over the top of the gravel and bend it up against the back of the stones. Fill the final inches with soil, packing it firmly.

⑤ Add the Top Layer

This wall has no capstones, but for a tidy look, it still needs a straight top edge. To create a reference line, stake mason's twine at the height you want. Then find stones that are as flat as possible on top and that fit well against the adjoining stones.

⑥ The End Result

The completed wall has stones that are level on top. They slant slightly toward the slope.

design lesson

>> A simple gauge allows you to check the wall's batter as you build. If you make the tool from 2 x 2s or 2 x 4s and tape, as shown, it will indicate a slope of about 1½ inches if the level is held plumb.

dry-stacked walls

A stacked stone wall fits naturally into the landscape, separating the path from a hillside planting bed.

Even though it lacks mortar, a dry-stacked stone wall can be amazingly durable. The key is in the stacking. The wall must be wider at the base than at the top so that each side presses into the other and keeps the wall upright (see tip on batter gauges on page 123). Experiment with different stones and orientations so that each piece rests solidly in place. Position two stones over one, or one stone over two, whenever possible. Choose stones that are at least partially squared off and flat on two sides. Bond stones, long enough to span the thickness of the wall, or at least reach much of the way through it, will give the wall much of its strength.

❶ Construct the Base Layer

Once the location has been determined and the site has been excavated (see page 121), begin with the footing. For a 2- to 3-foot-high wall, dig a 6- to 8-inch-deep trench, making it level on the bottom and a bit wider than your largest stones. Tamp the soil in the trench. Select large, flat stones, each about the same size, to give the wall a sturdy base. Place one layer of stones in the trench, fitting them together.

❷ Build the Wall

Add the next layer, staggering the stones so that the joints are not on top of each other. Backfill with gravel as each layer is added; by the time you reach the top third of the wall, switch to soil as a backfill material. Lightly tamp the soil at each layer to reduce settling. Keep in mind that the wall should batter into the slope approximately 1 inch for every foot of height to provide stability. Check periodically with a carpenter's level to make sure the wall is relatively level along its length. Make adjustments as you work, trying out stones of various sizes to help keep the wall level and filling gaps with small stones.

❸ Finishing

Set the top layer of stones in place. Check for level. Backfill behind the finished wall and tamp the soil, taking care not to compact it too much (this could put undue stress on the finished wall).

design lesson

The key to building an attractive stone wall is careful fitting. Properly placed, the stones make a harmonious and pleasing pattern, and the finished wall looks like a unit rather than a random pile of rocks. Stones can be stacked to create horizontal seams that line up, but long-running vertical seams weaken a dry-stacked wall and should be avoided.

freestanding walls

Dry-stacked walls are most often used as a way to contain soil and plants or to terrace a slope. But there are times when a freestanding stone wall is called for. The construction methods are similar to those for building a wall that faces outward; however, you'll want to ensure that the attractive character of each stone is showcased on both sides of the wall.

ABOVE: As a backdrop to the urn displayed in front of it, this dry-stacked wall is used as an accent in the garden rather than as part of a raised planting structure.

❶ Place the First Stones

Remove sod and all other organic material from an area about 3 inches wider than the wall's base perimeter. Scrape, rather than dig, the bottom of the excavation so that the stones will rest on undisturbed soil. Lay a bond stone at each end of the wall, as well as every 6 to 8 feet along its length. For this course, place the flattest side up. Excavate underneath or add gravel as needed so the stones seat firmly.

❷ Lay Additional Courses

As you continue to lay stones, keep the courses fairly even. Set large stones on each side and fill in the middle with small stones where needed. To ensure a stable wall, always lay one on top of two rather than stack stones of the same size directly on top of each other. Use a batter gauge (see page 123) to check that the wall leans slightly inward on both sides. Every few courses, add bond stones.

❸ Finish the Wall

Gently tap in small stones to fill gaps in the side of the wall and to keep larger pieces from wobbling. Finish the top with large, flat capstones that overhang the sides of the wall. Test that the capstones are fairly stable when rested on top. Make any necessary adjustments, then mix a batch of mortar and lay a 1- to 2-inch-thick bed. Press the capstones into the mortar.

How a Freestanding Wall Stays Up

A freestanding, dry-stacked stone wall gets its strength from its structure. Basically, it's a double retaining wall. Instead of battering into a slope, each side presses into the other and keeps the wall upright. The wall must always be wider at the base than at the top.

SUNSET CONTRIBUTING EDITOR
PETER O. WHITELEY ON

building a strong wall

>> Interconnect the front and back of the wall by placing a bond stone at both ends and every 6 to 8 feet along the wall's length. The spacing depends on the size of the stones you are using. If possible, use tie stones that span the wall's width. Otherwise, select pairs of stones that each reach three-fourths of the way through. Set them so they project inward from opposite sides and butt tightly.

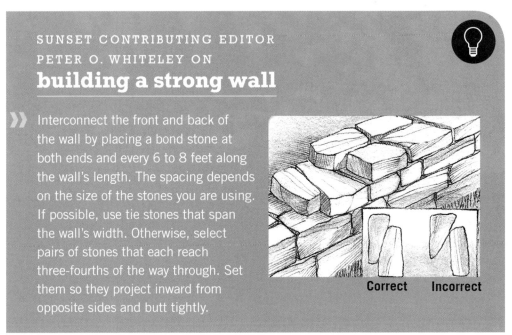

Correct   Incorrect

concrete footings

In contrast to a dry-laid wall's base of compacted gravel or even soil, most masonry walls need a concrete footing. A typical footing is 8 to 12 inches deep and twice as wide as the wall it will support. However, if the ground freezes where you live, local building codes may require a footing that extends below the frost line—the depth at which the soil freezes in your area. Where winters are mild, you may be able to use compacted gravel as a foundation. In the method shown on these pages, the walls of a carefully dug trench act as the form for the concrete.

ABOVE: Because of its height, this free-standing stucco-over-concrete-block wall was constructed on a concrete footing. The result is a safe and stable garden feature.

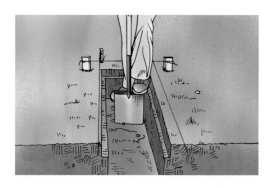

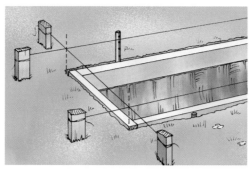

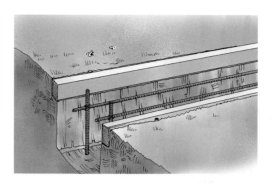

❶ Lay Out and Dig

Use mason's line and wood stakes to lay out the outside perimeter of the 2 x 4 frame that will go on top (step 2). If the wall is to turn a corner, check for square. Dig the hole with a square-bladed shovel. The top 3 inches of the hole should be 1½ inches wider in all directions than the main hole to accommodate the frame. Scrape, rather than dig, the bottom of the excavation and remove all loose soil so that the concrete will rest on undisturbed soil.

❷ Frame the Footing

Cut 2 x 4s for the frame, then screw them together at the corners. Check for square and level in all directions. Drive metal stakes to anchor the frame, as 2 x 4 stakes could cause the walls of the excavation to crumble. Drive the stakes below the tops of the 2 x 4s.

❸ Install Rebar

Local building codes may call for reinforcement bar, which increases the footing's ability to resist cracking if the soil underneath shifts. Typically, two horizontal pieces of ⅜-inch rebar are sufficient. To suspend the rebar in the center of the footing's depth, drive vertical pieces of rebar into the ground and wire the horizontal pieces to them.

❹ Pour and Screed

Mix concrete (see page 109) and pour it into the hole. A basic concrete mix works fine. Use a length of 2 x 4 to screed the top. Smooth the concrete with a magnesium or wood float.

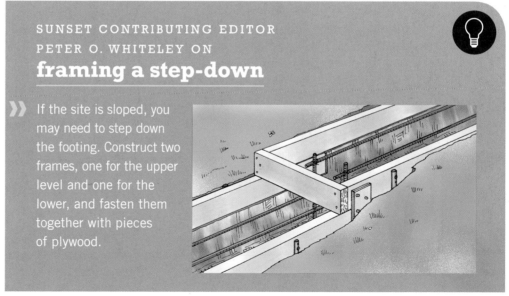

SUNSET CONTRIBUTING EDITOR
PETER O. WHITELEY ON
framing a step-down

❱❱ If the site is sloped, you may need to step down the footing. Construct two frames, one for the upper level and one for the lower, and fasten them together with pieces of plywood.

mortared walls

An attractive stone wall brings order to the surrounding landscape, creating a dramatic focal point.

A mortared stone wall can be narrower than a dry-stacked one and still be strong and stable, but it must rest on a solid concrete footing (see pages 128–129). Otherwise the mortar joints will crack as the soil heaves in frosts or settles over time. Make sure that your plan for the foundation meets local codes, which take into account regional weather conditions. Once the concrete footing is in place, proceed with the following steps.

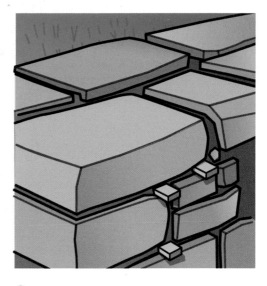

❶ Lay the First Course

Mix the mortar. Use a bagged mix or a homemade batch of 1 part masonry cement to 3 parts sand, plus just enough water to make a stiff mixture. Spread a 1-inch layer of mortar on the foundation and set the stones in place. Pack joints with mortar as you go, and wipe up any spills promptly with a damp sponge.

❷ Add Stones

Complete the first course, then add more layers. Set three or four stones in place and check that they rest without wobbling, then remove the stones, spread mortar, and replace the stones where they belong. Stagger joints and install bond stones (large enough to span the thickness of the wall) every 6 to 8 feet.

❸ Add Filler Stones

Fill gaps larger than 2 inches with small stones rather than mortar. If a stone sinks too deep into the mortar or wobbles, support it in one or two places by tapping in small wooden wedges. After the mortar stiffens, pull out the wedges and pack the holes with mortar.

❹ Rake the Joints

When you can press your thumb into the mortar and leave an impression without mortar sticking to your thumb, it's time to rake the joints. Shape the mortar between stones with a small scrap of wood or a pointing tool. If you wish, remove just enough mortar so that it is recessed slightly behind the face of the stones, working to produce joints that are consistent in depth.

❺ Finish the Wall

After raking, use a mason's brush to remove all mortar crumbs. If a stone is smeared with mortar, dampen a small towel and scrub the stone. Cover the wall with plastic for several days so that the mortar dries slowly. In dry or warm weather, lift the plastic and mist the wall periodically.

brick walls

A low, short garden wall is much stronger when it has at least two horizontal rows of bricks, called wythes. Patterns, or bonds, allow you to build double-wythe walls that interlock in various ways. Bricks turned sideways to tie the wythes together are called headers, while the other bricks are called stretchers. Most bonds require cutting (see page 89). To help you maintain rhythm and concentration as you throw mortar and lay bricks, cut a number of bricks in advance. See page 117 for tips on selecting the correct mortar for your project. Brick walls must rest atop a solid concrete footing (see pages 128–129).

ABOVE: This low brick wall creates an L-shaped raised planting bed in front of a high stuccoed wall. An adjacent path has brick edging to tie together the two garden elements.

❶ Lay the First Bricks

Prepare by first laying out bricks with ⅜-inch dowels between them to represent joints. Note how the bricks align at the corner. You may need to cut a brick or two. Mark the footings for the centers of each joint.

❷ Lay a Header Course

Starting at a corner or end of the wall, throw a line of mortar for the first three bricks. Then set and place the first brick. Butter one end of the next brick and set it. Push the bricks into place and see that the centers of the joints line up with your pencil marks. Check for level in both directions. Remove excess mortar. Repeat for the second wythe and lay bricks for the start of an adjoining wall if you are at a center. Check frequently with a level.

❸ Build a Lead

Continue building the corner or the end of the wall, which is called a lead. Make a stack seven or eight bricks high. As you go, use a level to check that the corner is plumb and the courses are level. Use a story pole, a measuring stake with marks indicating the center of each mortar joint, to check that each row is at the correct height. A standard model has marks every 8 inches to indicate three courses of common brick plus the mortar joints.

❹ String a Line Between Leads

Build a lead at the other end of the wall in the same way and check it with the story pole and level. Lay all the in-between bricks for the bottom course of both wythes, using the pencil lines as guides. Stretch a mason's line from one lead to the other at the center of a joint. The line should be taut and about ⅜ inch from the bricks.

❺ Fill In Between the Leads

For each course, move the line up one joint and use it as a guide for the height and for the outer edge of the wall. Don't let bricks touch the line. The last brick in the middle of a course, called the closure brick, is buttered at both ends. Butter it generously and slip it in straight down. You may need a striking tool to force more mortar into one joint.

❻ Strike the Joints

Every 20 minutes or so, depending on weather conditions, test the joints by pressing with your thumb. If a thumbprint holds its shape, it's time to strike. With a brick jointer, smooth all horizontal joints, then smooth the verticals so water will drain properly.

❼ Brush and Clean

Brush off excess mortar once it has started to harden and appears crumbly. If the mortar smears, stop and wait a few minutes longer. You may be able to wipe any smears away with a damp sponge, but take care not to get the joints very wet or you will weaken them. Alternatively, wait a day and then clean the wall with a mild muriatic acid solution.

concrete block walls

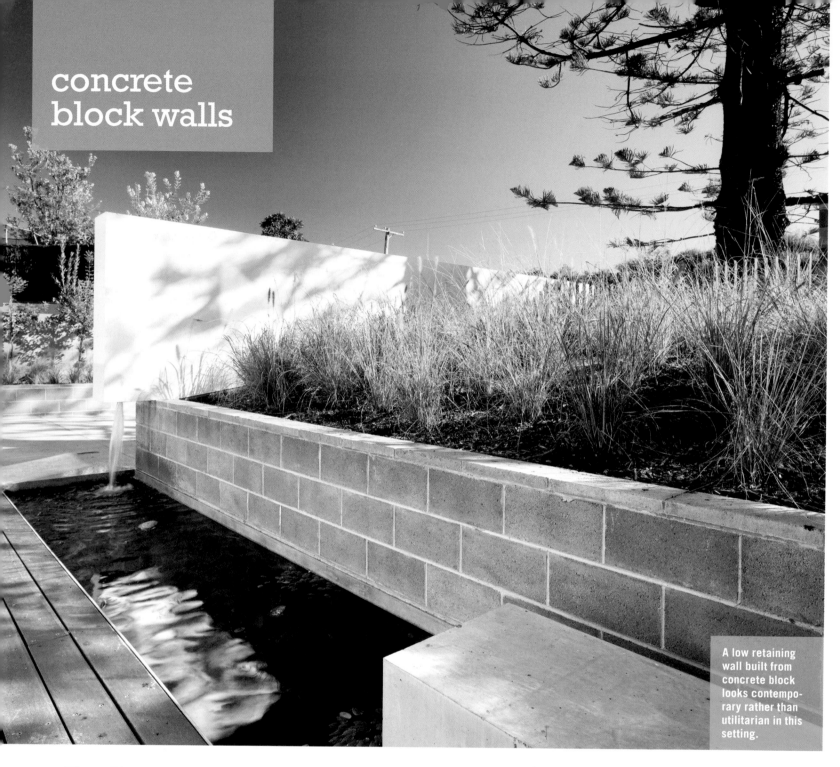

A low retaining wall built from concrete block looks contemporary rather than utilitarian in this setting.

Many concrete-block walls are made with blocks set in mortar beds, much like a brick wall. But there are easier options, including decorative interlocking blocks, which form a finished wall as soon as they are stacked, and surface-bonded concrete blocks, which consist of standard or special blocks that are stacked dry and then stuccoed.

Decorative interlocking blocks suitable for forming freestanding walls may require different installation methods than stone retaining walls (see page 123). Discuss your needs with a salesperson at a masonry supply company or home improvement center and read the instructions before you buy materials.

When coated with surface-bonding cement, concrete-block walls are actually stronger than walls built the conventional way. Sold in bags, surface-bonding cement contains fiber reinforcement as well as cement, fine sand, and polymers. You can buy special interlocking concrete blocks, or use standard ones for walls shorter than 3 feet. A surface-bonded wall must rest on a solid concrete foundation (see pages 128–129).

① Make Cuts

After the footing is installed, set a row of blocks in a dry run. Make any necessary cuts by scoring a line about ½ inch deep on each side with a circular saw fitted with a masonry or diamond blade. Finish the cut with a brick set or chisel and a mason's hammer.

② Lay the First Course

Mix a batch of surface-bonding cement and dampen the foundation. Spread the bonding cement as deep as the manufacturer recommends (generally, ⅛–½ inch). Set the first course of block in the cement. Use a solid-faced block at the end. Check for level.

③ Stack the Blocks

Stack the next courses so joints line up with every other course. Use a mason's line and level to check the wall as you go. If it's required by code, fill cells with an approved mortar. Shim where needed. If a block wobbles, stack the next course. If the weight of the blocks doesn't solve the problem, pick up the course, as well as the wobbly block. Trowel mortar on top of the block below and set the wobbly block back into place; tap with a hammer and a scrap of wood to settle the block at the same height as adjacent blocks.

④ Cap the Wall

For a square-looking top, finish the wall with interlocking cap blocks. If they are not available, spread surface-bonding mortar on top of the highest course and lay solid concrete pavers on the mortar.

⑤ Finishing

To apply surface-bonding mortar, begin by spraying the wall with water. Mix a small batch of surface-bonding cement and place it on a hawk (a flat-faced tool). Hold the hawk against the wall and trowel the cement upward. With the trowel nearly flat, press firmly to ensure a tight bond. Once you have covered an area of about 4 feet square, use long, sweeping strokes to smooth the surface. The surface-bonding mortar should be about ¼ inch thick. Rinse the trowel regularly, as a clean trowel is easier to use. To control cracking, use a concrete jointer to cut vertical control joints spaced about twice as far apart as the wall's height (for example, space them 6 feet apart on a 3-foot-high wall). Create a subtle texture by lightly running the trowel over the surface in sweeping motions. When applied lightly, a texture will not affect the control joints.

design lesson

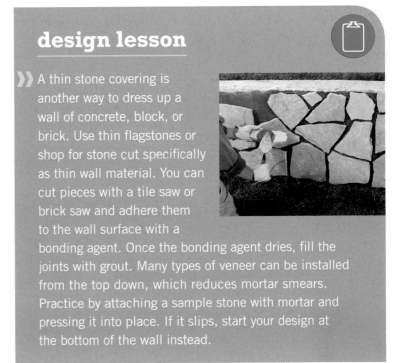

》 A thin stone covering is another way to dress up a wall of concrete, block, or brick. Use thin flagstones or shop for stone cut specifically as thin wall material. You can cut pieces with a tile saw or brick saw and adhere them to the wall surface with a bonding agent. Once the bonding agent dries, fill the joints with grout. Many types of veneer can be installed from the top down, which reduces mortar smears. Practice by attaching a sample stone with mortar and pressing it into place. If it slips, start your design at the bottom of the wall instead.

Finishing the Look

After considering the placement and purpose of pathways and walls in your garden and reviewing the steps and tools you'll need to create them, you're ready to select raw materials for the installation. Before you begin, however, you may want to consider decorative details that can personalize and enliven your exterior spaces. The addition of landscape lighting is another option to enhance your enjoyment and use of the garden after dusk. And, of course, you'll want to select the right plants that will accent the design of pathways and walls. Regard plants as the finishing touches that reflect your own design style. In this chapter, you'll find a wide range of options in all of these areas.

Your new path or wall project isn't complete until you've added flowers and foliage. Select plants that enhance the lines, materials, and placement of built elements, integrating them into the overall landscape.

define
your style

Ideally, three elements should combine to reveal the personality of the garden's owner: the constructed area (such as the blue-stone path, shown here), planting design (an informal arrangement of trees, perennials, and carpet roses), and the lifestyle details (a comfortable teak armchair and ottoman with a side table).

Landscape designers have been known to say that the garden is where "it's okay to break the rules." By this they mean that freedom of expression and experimentation are encouraged when you're creating the outdoor living environment. The garden can be a highly personal expression of who you are while also reflecting your lifestyle preferences (for example, whether you are casual or formal when you entertain guests). It can also take its design cues from the regional architecture and local geography—or a blend of all these factors.

But the most successful landscape designs are unified by what many garden-makers call hardscaping. The term generally refers to non-plant elements that give a garden its framework. That's why paths and walks, as well as garden walls, are essential to the overall look of your outdoor environment. As you evaluate what may already exist in your backyard and consider features to add, think about how these ingredients will contribute to the garden's appearance and function. Here are some design styles to inspire you.

Romantic

A simple gravel path gains a dreamy feeling, thanks to a double row of billowing lavender planted along its edges. The aromatic herb and the pleasing crunch of loose stone underfoot combine to transport this garden's occupants to the lavender fields of France.

Formal

The symmetrical lines of this perennial garden call for a formally designed pathway. Two orderly rows of stone pavers create a journey that is wide enough for visitors to walk side by side through the garden.

Asian/Zen

A raised walkway made of wooden planks, posts, and bamboo poles takes its inspiration from traditional Japanese and Chinese landscapes. The zigzag course creates a broken line that causes one to slow down and pay attention to the surrounding landscape.

Cottage/Country

A picket fence with a gate and arbor opens onto a cobblestone pathway and an exuberant cutting garden. These carefree design ingredients are some of the favorites of cottage- and country-style landscapes.

Modern/Contemporary

Simple geometry and repetition give this pathway a modern sensibility. Horizontal bands of concrete that alternate with unfussy ground cover plants reinforce the design.

Beach/Meadow

Planks of stone create steps and a path that leads through a semi-wild meadow of grass to the distant shore. The unconstructed design is well suited to this naturalistic setting.

Rustic/Woodland

Both the soft mulch and the meandering lines of this path are suitable for a woodland shade garden. Anyone who ventures here will be offered a quiet, contemplative journey.

Whimsical

A playful mix of materials and interlocking shapes add up to a light-hearted space in the garden. Together, the artful installation and the hidden destination foster a sense of curiosity for those who wander along this pathway.

There's a wild-desert feeling to the colors and shapes of the plants that border this stripped-down path. Individual concrete pads create the illusion that they're hovering above the desert floor. Their exposed aggregate finish blends in with the native soil's stony texture.

get creative

Granite cubes are set into a base of sand to form a circular detail that contrasts nicely with a brick path.

When you are planning a path, walkway, or wall, the primary consideration will be to assess the area's scale and choose materials as they relate to the property's architecture and style. Don't overlook the small but significant ways you can personalize your paths and walls. Decorative details can be expressed as subtle accents or exuberant artwork. Take advantage of construction opportunities to insert contrasting materials, play with geometric shapes, and create patterns by simply rearranging rectangular brick or paver shapes like pieces of a quilt.

Bold Square

A square-within-a-square pattern is created with specially cut stone pavers.

Dramatic Diamonds

A diamond-patterned pathway is made with square-cut stone. The design's background is formed by irregular pieces of flagstone laid on edge.

Circular Accent

Preformed cast stone sections are easy to assemble into a circular focal point in a gravel path. The circle suggests a gathering point, much like an area rug in the center of a living room.

BEAUTIFUL BRICK Re-imagine everyday brick into artfully expressed surfaces.

Timeless Patina

Recycled brick in a spectrum of pale to dark shades is laid in a zigzag pattern to enliven the entry path.

Point of View

Some of the standard bricks used in this design have been cut to create this bold circular detail that intersects the pathway.

Beyond Ordinary

These bricks are installed on edge to expose their thinner sides, which is an attractive way to make a herringbone pattern.

An alternating pattern created by three horizontal bricks and a vertical one creates an attractive border along a gravel path.

decorative concrete

Off-the-shelf square concrete pavers take on a serene beauty when paired with smooth pebbles in this Zen garden.

Concrete is a durable choice for hardworking paths, walks, and walls. But it need not be plain or industrial in appearance. You can add color, create a flagstone-like appearance using stamping tools, combine concrete with natural materials for interesting patterns, or assemble a prefabricated kit into a decorative feature. One way to ensure that your creation is a success is to assemble a sample first. You can install it on top of a heavy plastic tarp or onto bare soil, perhaps in an obscure area of the yard. Experiment with pigments and added textures (such as aggregate stone) this way as well.

CREATIVE AND COMPLEMENTARY Concrete pairs well with stone and brick.

Two-Tone Scheme

Standard concrete pavers are paired here with brick-colored concrete to build an informal walkway in a perennial garden. The design contrasts nicely with gravel mulch in the same palette.

Perfect Fit

Irregularly shaped concrete steppingstones allow passage alongside this brick patio. Such concrete pavers can be purchased as a fit-together kit or poured in place using a cookie-cutter-style template.

Durable Finish

Tumbled concrete squares, sometimes called Roman pavers, create a tidy, easy-to-navigate walkway. This affordable and widely available material is usually sold in standard gray or brick shades.

Patchwork Paving

A secret outdoor dining area uses recycled concrete as its floor. Because these pieces were formerly part of a patio or driveway, their thickness is uniform, which makes installation easier.

Duo-Tone Surface

An entry walk gains interesting textures and patterns with two concrete-colored materials. The larger square pavers alternate with rows of brick-shaped concrete cobbles to reveal a tone-on-tone design.

Three in One

A curved concrete path mixes aggregate edges, smooth concrete in the center, and pigmented diamonds that lead to the greenhouse beyond.

Floating Bands

This contemporary walk features preformed bands of concrete and a variety of smooth pebbles.

Open Grid

Pervious concrete pavers form a path that is environmentally friendly, safe, and walkable.

This design features concrete that was treated with a natural stone pigment. A paper stencil was used to create the look of grout lines, and the surface was dusted with multicolored sand for extra texture. The technique can be an affordable alternative to laying stone pavers or flagstone paths.

shopping for supplies

Together, crushed rock, pebbles, and strips of wood make a dynamic walkway.

On the following pages, you'll find brief descriptions of the materials available for most paths, walkways, and garden wall projects. Whether you plan to build with a natural material such as gravel or flagstone or a manufactured option like brick or concrete, there is a diverse selection of ingredients to choose from. Familiarize yourself with the terminology and best use of each, then visit local suppliers, including stone yards and home and garden centers, to obtain samples and compare costs.

If possible, when using stone in a wall or path, choose a type considered local to your area; it will look more natural than an exotic variety shipped from far away. Local sources of stone and other materials such as crushed rock are also likely to be less expensive because of lower transportation costs. Don't overlook salvage yards that recycle brick and other building materials and check classified ads or online sources. You may be surprised to find just what you're looking for at a considerable savings.

GRAVEL, PEBBLES, AND SAND Use for informal paths or base rock.

Sand

Sand is used as the subsurface to dry-laid brick, cobblestone, or flag-stone paths. Consult a local stone yard to determine the right type of sand for your installation. It may be called torpedo sand, leveling sand, concrete sand, or screen-ings of a certain type of stone. Screened limestone is not recom-mended, as it will leach alkaline into soil, potentially damaging grass or plants.

Gravel

These small stones are either collected from natural deposits or crushed from larger pieces. Gravel can be purchased by the grade. For example, "quarter-minus" grade describes pieces that measure one-quarter inch or less.

Decomposed Granite

Finely ground granite is also called DG. While it is as fine in texture as sand, individual pieces have flat rather than rounded composi-tion, which allows the material to pack firmly for an easy-to-walk-on surface.

Decorative Pebbles

Depending on your area, decorative pebbles will reflect the native stone. Unlike crushed rock, which has sharp edges, pebbles are smooth and range from pea- to plum-sized. Alone, this material isn't that comfortable as a walking surface. However, it is very attrac-tive when combined with a path of stable steppingstones.

SUNSET HEAD GARDENER
RICK LAFRENTZ ON
designing with loose material

>> Decomposed granite and gravel are often considered for informal or casual path construction. However, with attention to detail, such as adding small pieces of flagstone as edging, a path made of loose material gains definition and interest. The outline of this artful path is contained by edging stones that reinforce the irregular design. A half-inch layer of decomposed granite laid over a compacted surface forms the central path, while larger gravel and varying sizes of smooth stones contrast along the edges, where cactus and succulent plantings emerge.

STONE FOR PATHS AND WALLS For workability as well as appearance.

Steppingstones
Whether they're flat-topped field stones or thicker flagstones, steppingstones have a slightly irregular, nonslip surface and come in manageable sizes, which makes them just right for paths.

Cut Stone
Sometimes called stone tile, this is a formal-looking material suitable for a wide variety of projects. Pieces are cut into squares or rectangles, each with a flat back and sawn edges. The top surface may be smooth (honed) or textured (uncut).

Cobblestones
Usually carved from granite into roughly uniform cubes or brick shapes, cobblestones are easy to work with. They make excellent paths and path edgings.

Flagstone
Large, flat slabs of varying thicknesses, flagstones are irregular in shape and often have a slightly rough surface for good traction. For use as steppingstones or wider walkways laid on a sand bed, choose stones that are 1½ inches thick or more. Thinner flagstones will need to be laid in wet mortar or concrete.

Rubble
These are irregularly shaped wall stones, whether fieldstones or small boulders. They have a natural look, but their random shapes make them a challenging material to build with.

Semi-dressed Stone
These pieces have been roughly trimmed so that they are mostly flat on two sides. This makes them easier to use for building walls, but they still have a rugged, somewhat informal look.

Ashlar
Fully trimmed and formal-looking, these block-shaped stones stack easily. The ashlar stones shown above can be used to construct rows of the same height. Other configurations use stones of varying heights.

Natural Veneer Stone
These stones are specially cut into uniformly thick, flat-backed pieces for facing concrete walls. Lightweight, they are easy to set into mortar. They also work well stacked as path edging and for walls around raised planting beds.

Two stone-building techniques create an attractive corner detail. The dry-stacked fieldstone forms a raised planting bed, while cut pavers assemble a pathway.

Concrete blocks
form an accent
wall that encloses
this entry garden.
It has been
painted slate gray
to echo the stone
pavers.

CONCRETE, FABRICATED STONE, AND STUCCO   Durable and affordable for walls and paths.

Concrete Cobbles

Tumbled and colored to mimic the look of weathered stone, concrete cobblestones are available in various sizes and shapes. You can also buy easy-to-install sets that create circular or fan-shaped patterns.

Concrete Pavers

These may be interlocking paving units that resemble bricks or large rectangular, round, or hexagonal pieces with or without exposed aggregate on the surface. They are designed to fit together as pavers without mortar.

Concrete Blocks

Concrete blocks usually have two large holes, or cells, that you leave open or fill with mortar for extra strength. Standard concrete blocks are listed as 8 inches high by 8 inches wide by 16 inches long. Pieces are actually ⅜ inch smaller in each dimension to account for mortar space. Half blocks and corner pieces are also available.

Stackable Retaining Blocks

This concrete material interlocks without mortar to form a wall solid enough to keep a slope or a garden bed firmly in place. Easy to install and widely available, the material may be rectangular for straight walls or trapezoidal for curves.

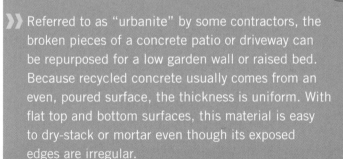

Manufactured Veneer

Designed as a wall facing, this material is made from lightweight aggregates in panel form or from very thin pieces of natural stone laminated onto composite materials. They are flat-backed for facing concrete walls with mortar.

Stucco

Modern stucco is an exterior cement-plaster facing material that can be applied to flat or curved surfaces, such as concrete block walls. Stucco's appearance can be varied with the application tools used and with the addition of aggregates and pigments. It is a durable wall cover in most any climate.

design lesson

Referred to as "urbanite" by some contractors, the broken pieces of a concrete patio or driveway can be repurposed for a low garden wall or raised bed. Because recycled concrete usually comes from an even, poured surface, the thickness is uniform. With flat top and bottom surfaces, this material is easy to dry-stack or mortar even though its exposed edges are irregular.

Vintage Brick

Recycled or used bricks, which often have bits of mortar stuck on the surface, add a rustic look to garden projects. If there are remnants of mortar on all faces of old brick, it probably means the material was used indoors and is less likely to be weatherproof or suitable for paving. You can also find new yet distressed brick that looks vintage and comes with a weather rating.

Standard Brick

Paving bricks are always solid, made from clay or shale. They measure 4 by 8 by 2¼ inches and can be used for paving where pieces have ⅛ inch of sand between the joints. They're also good edging pieces for paths. Bricks rated SW (for severe weathering) can be used in all climates.

Modular Brick

If you intend to use mortar between joints, buy modular-sized bricks, which are typically 3⅝ by 7⅝ inches. You can then have ⅜-inch-wide mortar joints and create patterns that line up correctly. These bricks have slightly rounded, or chamfered, edges, which aid in slip resistance and allow water to drain better.

Concrete Brick

This material is tinted and molded to look like clay bricks. It costs less and can be used in the same ways as clay-based brick. Over time, concrete bricks may lighten. Also, sand in the concrete mix may become exposed, changing the look.

Brick Veneer

This type of thin brick is designed to be added as a surface over concrete block walls, poured concrete, or even wood. Brick veneer pieces are cut to expose the side dimension so the finished wall looks as if it were built of solid brick. Some manufacturers make special corner pieces that hide the thin veneer edge.

A running-bond installation of recycled brick follows the lines of this generous entry path.

Narrow aggregate pavers are placed two at a time with strips of clipped grass in between, creating a rhythmic pathway.

158

Metal

Ornamental and industrial metal pieces can be creative accents when paired with organic wall and path elements. Architectural salvage and recycled metal are suitable as a pathway edging material or to create a wall ledge.

Wood

Choose wood that reflects your home's architectural finish and use it to define the edge of a pathway or in combination with other wall materials. Thinner, bendable wood can be curved to outline a raised bed or contain a loose gravel or pebble pathway. Wooden boards laid in gravel create a boardwalk-inspired path, as illustrated here.

Glass

Recycled and tumbled glass is often available from garden centers and stone yards. It can be found in a spectrum of colors and be used as a substitute for gravel in a steppingstone path. It can also be incorporated into a more intricate mosaic pattern on walkable surfaces.

Tile

Outdoor-grade terra-cotta, ceramic, or porcelain tile is a good choice for paths or for adding accent color to walls and walks. In most cases, tiles must be set in a bed of thinset mortar atop a solid concrete slab. The spaces between tiles should be grouted. Recycled or broken tile is an ingredient in mosaic-patterned walls and walks.

lighting the garden

Dining al fresco is a thoroughly romantic activity, thanks to the use of up-lighting that showcases the trees around the garden's perimeter. Votive candles decorate and illuminate the tabletop.

The worst landscape lighting resembles that of airport runways, with twin rows of bulbs on either side of a central path. Do-it-yourself light kits can have a short lifespan because of inexpensive materials, and some solar-powered lighting systems shine so dimly that they are ineffective as the main light source. The best landscape lighting is both dramatic and functional. Look for durable, low-voltage systems that run on 12-volt power with a small transformer that can be plugged into a standard outdoor receptacle. The most important places to light after dark are paths, planting areas or garden beds, walls or fences, and trees.

Directional Lighting

A pathway is lit by a series of glass hurricanes that hold small candles. While temporary, the lights convey festivity for an evening in the garden.

Spotlights in Path

Upward-facing spotlights are installed at the base of bamboo plants. You may not notice the light source as much as the shadow play of foliage against the dramatic red wall.

Up-Lighting

There are numerous low-voltage up-light fixtures that can throw attention-grabbing highlights against plants. Typically, these lights are designed to be semi-obscure at the base of trunks or hidden by foliage.

Wall-Mounted Fixtures

A decorative fixture attached to a flat plate for easy installation on a garden wall reflects the garden's style and throws plenty of light after dark. Mountable wall lighting is widely available and should echo other materials used in the landscape.

Light Posts

Low-voltage fixtures are an ideal solution for illuminating the edge of a garden path or as directional aids elsewhere in the landscape. Because the post elevates the lamp 10 to 12 inches above ground level, this style lights both a walkway and surrounding plants. You can find similar landscape lighting kits that include a programmable transformer and all the necessary cables and connections.

Decorative Lanterns

Glass jars used as votive candle holders are suspended from overhead tree branches to create a playful installation. This is an easy and attractive way to bring light into the garden after sunset.

plants
for paths

Tufts of ornamental sedge seem to emerge randomly from the carpet of soft mosses and a casual stepping-stone path.

When planning the paths and walkways of your garden, don't overlook the role of plants as an essential design element. The diverse world of ground covers, grasses, vines, bulbs, and other plants with unique path-hugging habits helps to embroider the ground plane and make it highly interesting. When choosing plants to add along a path's edge, remember that softer is better. Thorns, spines, barbs, and anything stiff are unwelcome to pant legs and ankles. When choosing plants to install directly into the path's surface, think about durability and scale. Ground covers and low-growing plants do not have to be completely flat; however, they do need to withstand gentle foot traffic over time. Make your path a focal point by choosing plants that are compatible with the site and pleasing to the senses (visually or aromatically) and that are generally easy-care varieties requiring infrequent pruning or deadheading.

FOR GARDEN FLOORS Create a planted path or walk.

Filling Spaces Between Pavers

Look for proven, durable, evergreen ground covers adapted to your growing region—ones that can withstand the occasional footsteps and are short enough to be unobtrusive. Attractive, low-growing perennials, herbs, and mosses are available, including aubrieta, baby's tears (*Selaginella* sp., pictured here), blue star creeper, brass buttons (*Leptinella squalida*), carpet bugle, chamomile, *Dichondra*, dwarf mondo grass, green carpet (*Herniaria glabra*), Irish and Scotch moss, Korean grass (*Zoysia tenuifolia*), *Mazus reptans*, woolly thyme, woolly yarrow, and low-growing sedums, speedwells, and violets.

Softening Hard Edges

Plants that cascade, arch, creep, and billow are good edge softeners. Ferns, ornamental grasses, dwarf shrubs, and many bulbs grow companionably next to the contours of a pathway. Examples include false spirea (*Astilbe*, pictured here), *Aeonium*, agapanthus, bleeding heart, cinquefoil, daphne, *Echeveria*, gentian, heath (*Erica*), *Sempervivum*, low-growing junipers, meadowsweet (*Filipendula*), Jerusalem sage (*Phlomis*), *Dianthus*, rockrose (*Cistus*), Russian sage (*Perovskia*), Scotch heather, St. Johnswort, sunrose (*Helianthemum nummularium*), cranesbill (*Geranium*), and wall flower (*Erysimum*).

Adding Color and Texture

Elevate the most humble of path surfaces with a burst of soft-looking, relatively low-growing perennials that consistently provide form or bloom color. Try African daisy (*Osteospermum*), aster, begonia, blue marguerite (*Felicia amelloides*), chrysanthemum, cinquefoil, sea pink (*Armeria martima*), common geranium (*Pelargonium*), coral bells, daylily, dead nettle, false spirea (*Astilbe*), gazania, lady's mantle, *Erigeron*, pansy, petunia, Serbian bellflower, snow-in-summer, cranesbill (*Geranium*), twinspur, and verbena. For seasonal contrast, incorporate clipped boxwood forms and spring-blooming bulbs.

Growing in a Gravel Garden

Perennials and grasses that emerge from gravel pathways are reminiscent of carefree Mediterranean settings. You can create this look by selecting drought-tolerant plants that thrive in sunny, well-drained areas (while you generally don't need to worry about plants getting too soggy in a gravel path, they will heat up quickly from reflective heat). Try *Agastache*, agave, aloe, Apache plume (*Fallugia paradoxa*), blanket flower, coreopsis, daffodil, evening primrose (*Oenothera*), gaura, lamb's ears, globe mallow, lavender, penstemon, red valerian, red yucca (*Hesperaloe parviflora*), rock rose (*Cistus*), sage, *Santolina*, stonecrop, verbena, yarrow, and yucca.

SUNSET GARDEN EDITOR
KATHLEEN NORRIS BRENZEL ON
how to buy ground covers

》 Many people are used to purchasing ground-cover plants in 4-inch nursery pots, but the price can add up if a large surface area needs to be covered. As a penny-saving alternative, buy ground covers in flats (2-by-3-foot planting trays), or ask your garden center to order them for you. These plants can be teased apart easily and planted as small clumps (plant, root, and soil together). You'll need to water frequently during the first season to make sure these tiny sections do not dry out.

Shading a Path

To make a path feel welcoming and intimate, you will want to plant a variety of trees, shrubs, and perennials that relate to the scale of your home. Look for deciduous trees that provide shade in summer and allow winter light to penetrate the entry area when their branches are bare. Trees should have noninvasive roots and be relatively litter-free (fruit and flowers can be beautiful, but when they fall, it may increase garden maintenance). Consider a smaller or slow-growing tree that will not outpace the planting area, such as the many wonderful varieties of Japanese maple. Other attractive choices include crape myrtle, dogwood, flowering cherry, flowering crabapple, juneberry (*Amelanchier*), small magnolias, small maples, palo verde (*Cercidium*), Persian parrotia, redbud, smoke tree (*Cotinus*), sourwood, and *Stewartia*. Evergreen trees will provide year-round shade and interest, as well, including bronze loquat, citrus, small types of cypress, *Michelia*, fruitless forms of olive, smaller palms, fern pine (*Podocarpus*), and evergreen pear.

Enhancing Garden Steps

Paths occasionally also handle grade changes, such as steps or terraces. Knowing what to grow along the edges of a flight of steps (or even directly into the treads or risers of a staircase) requires an approach similar to planting a path (see page 162). Choose durable plants that are drought-tolerant, can grow in tight spaces, and can handle a little foot traffic. Ground covers, trailing herbs, cascading perennials, and ornamental grasses are useful to de-emphasize an imposing installation of steps or to integrate a smaller staircase into the overall garden scheme. Choices include artemisia, Australian fuchsia (*Correa*), clumping bamboo, bottlebrush (*Callistemon*), breath of heaven (*Coleonema*), cape plumbago, cotoneaster, crape myrtle, heath, lavender, manzanita, ninebark (*Physocarpus*), Pride of Madeira (*Echium candicans*), rockrose (*Cistus*), rosemary, snowberry (*Symphoricarpos*), salal (*Gaultheria shallon*), santolina, shrubby dogwoods (*Cornus*), sunrose (*Helianthemum nummularium*), toyon (*Heteromeles arbutifolia*), flowering thyme (seen here), muhly grass (*Muhlenbergia rigens*), needle grass (*Nassella tenuissima*), and sedge (*Carex buchananii*). Many climbing vines (see page 167) will also scramble nicely along the edge of a staircase.

Planting for Designs and Patterns

Compact, tufted, or small-leafed plants can create attractive designs in a pathway. When established, these tidy ground covers and grasses paint a pattern of color and texture in the negative spaces between stones, pavers and bricks. As you design the garden floor, use plants to give it a graphic punch, such as the grid of green that fuses the square pavers shown here. Scented plants, including herbs like thyme and Corsican mint, will release a pleasing aroma when stepped on. By alternating bright and dark green ground covers (such as Irish and Scotch mosses), you can emulate a woven blanket—another way to enliven pathways. Examples of pattern-making plants include Bugleweed (*Ajuga reptans*), Lady's mantle, Canadian wild ginger (*Asarum canadense*), dwarf hostas, *Lamium galeobdolon*, saxifrage, nasturtium, periwinkle (*Vinca minor*), yarrow, chamomile, oregano varieties (*Origanum majorana* and *O. vulgare*), lamb's ears, garden thyme, dianthus varieties, *Epimedium*, *Lewisia rediviva*, and Forget-me-not (*Myosotis sylvatica*). Plants in the mint family, including spearmint and peppermint, can be invasive unless planted where they are constrained by paving material.

Growing Near a Swimming Pool

When choosing plants to grow near a pool or spa, you should use the same rules as if designing a planting scheme for the path: Avoid thorny or spiked plants that will potentially scratch pedestrians. Look for plants that are smooth or velvety. You should design for easy maintenance, selecting perennials, shrubs, grasses, and trees that drop very little litter (or choose plants whose leaf or flower debris is too large to enter the pool's filter). Consider camellia, *Aeonium*, *Agave attenuata*, bird of paradise, canna, cordyline, *Cyperus*, daylily, edible fig, elephant's ear, fortnight lily (*Dietes*), ginger lily (*Hedychium*), honey bush (*Melianthus*), hydrangea, jade plant, Japanese auralia (*Fatsia japonica*), kangaroo paw (*Anigozanthos*), lily turf (*Liriope*), New Zealand flax, ornamental banana, palms, pineapple guava, tobira (*Pittosporum tobira*), *Schefflera*, sea lavender (*Limonium perezii*), Texas olive (*Cordia boissieri*), and tree ferns.

plants for garden walls

Growing along the top edge of a stone wall, delicate blue flowers add interest and contrast to the architecture.

Even though "vertical gardening" feels new and hip, in fact, growing plants on retaining walls and terraces is an age-old technique seen in many cultures and locales. The appeal is universal today, as well. Vines can obscure an unattractive wall or improve the surface of a plain one. Small plants often thrive in the cracks and crevices of stone or brick walls (see opposite page). An increasing selection of columnar trees, developed by the nursery trade, are ideal for slender spaces. They may be just the solution to enhance an ordinary garden wall. For retaining walls and terraces, a cascade of flowers or foliage adds charm as well as a softening effect.

Install plants so their branches and foliage will brush over the wall's upper edge. Plants that thrive in well-drained conditions are ideal for wall plantings. You will also want to select plants that can handle the heat absorbed by stone, brick, and concrete in summer. Choose quick-growing perennials and annuals with a spreading or low mounding shape, such as aubretia, bacopa, creeping Jenny, *Euphorbia*, garden nasturtium, *Hebe*, *Impatiens walleriana*, ivy geranium (*Pelargonium*), rose moss (*Portulaca grandiflora*), *Saponaria*, *Scaevola*, Serbian bellflower, sweet alyssum, and trailing types of petunia, twinspur, and verbena. Alternatively, plant low-growing or spreading shrubs like cotoneaster, *Euonymus fortunei*, juniper (shown here), hydrangea (shown here), trailing lantana, lavender, and carpet roses (as shown above).

FOR VERTICAL SURFACES Add plants to enhance walls, terraces, and hillsides.

Climbing a Wall

Some vines and climbing plants attach themselves firmly to a wall surface with sucker-like holdfasts or aerial roots. Often called clinging vines, these include climbing hydrangea, creeping fig, ivy, and *Parthenocissus* (seen here), which clambers the facade of a stone retaining wall to create a timeless focal point in the landscape. Other vines scramble up the wall or use its surface for support, or they may twine around or hook onto protrusions with their tendrils. Some favorite choices in this category are Carolina jessamine (*Gelsemiium sempervirens*), cat's claw (*Macfadyena unguis-cati*), clematis, climbing roses, honeysuckle, jasmine, morning glory, nasturtium, ornamental grape (*Vitis*), and sweet pea.

Planting at the Foot of a Wall

The selection of plants for the base of a wall can be determined by its garden orientation. Heat-loving plants like the succulents shown above are content to bake against a wall that faces south or west. Shade-loving plants appreciate protection on the north or east side of a terrace or garden wall. Choose compact, mounding, or cascading forms to spread along a wall and onto an adjacent path. Some good choices include sedges (*Carex* sp.), coral bells (*Heuchera* sp.), hostas, succulents, creeping rosemary, lavender, and lamb's ears.

Filling Wall Crevices

A surprising variety of plants will grow well in the niches of dry-laid walls and those built from recycled concrete or old brick. To get the greenery started, line the largest wall gaps with pieces of sphagnum moss, fill with a small amount of potting soil, insert the roots, and water lightly. Small ferns, mosses, and woodland perennials will thrive in shaded walls, creating a grotto-like effect. For walls in the sun, the many choices include cheddar pink (*Dianthus gratianopolitanus*), cranesbill (*Geranium*), Dalmatian bellflower (*Campanula porten-* *schlagiana*), Euphorbia myrsinites, Echeveria, globe daisy, houseleek (*Sempervivum*), ice plant, *Lewisia*, oregano, rockcress (*Arabis*), Santa Barbara daisy, sea pink (*Armeria martima*), sedum, Spanish lavender (small varieties), stone cress (*Aethionema*), trailing phlox (*Phlox nivalis*), and creeping thymes (shown here).

---

design lesson

›› Give your wall plantings some help with a trellis system. Depending on the material used to build your wall, there are several options for supporting the plants that grow against or along its surface. Choose a trellising framework that complements the design.

 » If your wall is constructed of brick or concrete block, install a grid or fine cable wire with masonry hardware. Be sure to use hardware that creates space behind the trellis, allowing vines or climbing roses room to grow.

 » If you plan on training woody plants into an espalier pattern against a wall, construct a trellis to support that design. A diamond or square grid pattern built of 1-by-1-inch wood should be built far enough away from the wall to allow good air circulation, especially for fruit-bearing plants.

 » Simple bamboo stakes can be installed in front of a wall to aid climbing annuals, such as sweet pea vines or nasturtiums, to scramble up a cobblestone or dry-stacked wall. Once the vines anchor themselves to the stone, the stakes can be pulled out and saved for future use.

FOR WALLS AND TERRACES   Select plants that add dimension and interest.

Trees for Walls

A trio of potted trees—in this case, Portugal laurels (*Prunus lusitanica*) trained onto standard trunks—can enhance an otherwise prosaic concrete or stucco wall. The trees' foliage is elevated enough so that it won't be hit by heads or shoulders of any passersby. Columnar trees are also a good choice to plant along a garden wall, since they have been trained, pruned, or bred to grow in narrow spaces. Some options include arborvitae (*Thuja occidentalis* 'Fastigiata' or *T. o.* 'Pyramidalis'), clumping bamboo, fern pine (*Podocarpus gracilior*), Irish juniper, skyrocket juniper (*Juniperus scopulorum* 'Skyrocket'), Italian cypress, fruitless olive, or yew.

Pairing Plants with Walls

When it comes to designing for impact, less can be more, such as this combination of a peacock blue stuccoed wall and flowering hostas. This focal point is successful because the use of a single ornamental plant massed against the intensely colored wall is both simple and sophisticated. There are as many different design combinations as there are plants and walls. Plants with bold foliage shapes or variegated colorations are good choices, such as Aralia ivy (x *Fatshedera*), black locust (*Robinia pseudoacadia* 'Frisia'), blue atlas cedar (*Cedrus atlantica* 'Glauca Pendula'), boxleaf honeysuckle (*Lonicera nitida*), flowering dogwood (*Cornus florida*), ginkgo, heavenly bamboo (*Nandina domestica*), hornbeam (*Carpinus caroliniana*), honey bush (*Melianthus major*), Japanese laurel (*Aucuba japonica*), Japanese maples, katsura (*Cercidiphyllum japonicum*), Japanese mock orange (*Pittosporum tobira*), leucothoe, lily-of-the-valley bush (*Pieris japonica*), magnolia, ninebark (*Physocarpus opulifolius*), oakleaf hydrangea (*Hydrangea quercifolia*), Persian ironwood (*Parrotia persica*), redbud (*Cercis canadensis* 'Forest pansy'), rice paper plant (*Tetrapanax papyrifer*), smoke bush (*Cotinus coggygria* 'Royal Purple'), sourwood (*Oxydendrum arboreum*), sweet gum (*Liquidambar*), and tupelo (*Nyssa sylvatica*).

Espaliered Plants for Walls

The technique of training trees and shrubs along a two-dimensional, vertical surface is called *espalier*. While a classic method of growing fruit trees in small spaces, espaliered ornamental trees, roses, or shrubs are also visually unique. When branches are trained into horizontal, L-shaped fan patterns or a beautiful diamond design called a Belgian Fence, they add a special element to your garden wall. Citrus trees, such as the one seen here, can also be gently encouraged to spread branches across the flat plane. The branches are either pruned gradually to the desired shape or trained along a cable or trellis using ties. If you wish to add this decorative green layer to a wall, look for pre-trained trees and shrubs offered at garden centers. Apple, pear, Italian plum, and citrus varieties are good espaliered trees. Firethorn (*Pyracantha*) is stunning when trained along a wall, while several varieties of climbing and caning roses will also respond well to this method.

Mounting Wall-Hanging Containers

As with any interior wall, the vertical surfaces of your garden offer a blank canvas for ornamentation. Pottery, artwork and container plants are attractive wall embellishments, especially when hung at eye level or enjoyed from the vantage point of a comfortable bench. Combine flat-backed planters or boxes with decorative tiles or plaques, as seen here, for an outdoor gallery-style installation. Wall-hanging containers may not be heavy by themselves, but with the addition of potting soil, roots, and moisture, they can be weighty. With this in mind, mount a wall planter using masonry hardware designed for a weight range much heavier than the pot. The container needs at least one drainage hole, ideally positioned slightly forward so dripping water won't run down the wall surface. Consider using plants that can withstand periods without moisture, such as sedums, succulents, and small cactuses. If you want to enjoy the explosion of cascading color produced by annuals and tender perennials, plan on watering wall containers daily in summer. Good choices include alyssum, bacopa (*Sutera cordata*), begonia, candytuft, coleus, *Cerinthe major*, dichondra, geranium, heliotrope, impatiens, lantana, licorice vine, lobelia, million bells (*Calibrichoa*), monkey flower (*Mimulus* x *hybridus*), nasturtium, painted tongue (*Salpiglosis sinuata*), pelargonium, petunia, Santa Barbara daisy (*Erigeron karavinskianus*), sweet potato vine, tickseed (*Coreopsis*), twinspur (*Diascia*), *Verbena* x *hybridus*, or vinca.

resources

The following is a list of organizations, manufacturers, and retail sources that you might find helpful in creating your new path, walkway, or wall. Whenever possible, we encourage you to patronize suppliers in your own community and those dedicated to environmentally responsible manufacturing processes and products.

To find a local supplier, check the online sources listed here for dealers in your area, or look in the Yellow Pages under these headings: Stone—Natural, Stone—Landscaping, Quarries, Rock, Building Materials, Masonry, Gravel and Sand, Landscape Equipment and Supplies.

Organizations and Associations

American Nursery and Landscape Association
www.anla.org
202-789-2900

American Society of Landscape Architects
www.asla.org
888-999-2752

Association of Professional Landscape Designers
ww.apld.org
717-238-9780

Building Materials Reuse Association
www.buildingreuse.org
800-990-2672

The Masonry Advisory Council
www.maconline.org
847-297-6704
Provides information about masonry design and products

Portland Cement Association
www.cement.org
847-966-6200
Provides resources and information about North American cement suppliers

Materials, Stone, and Construction Products

Advanced Pavement Technology
www.advancedpavement.com
877-882-3071
Permeable paver systems

Allan Block Corporation
www.allanblock.com
952-835-5309
Stackable block for retaining walls and vertical walls

Bourget Bros.; Bourget Flagstone Co.
www.bourgetbros.com
310-450-6556
Natural stone, tile, pebbles, and custom building materials

Buechel Stone Corporation
www.buechelstone.com
800-236-4473
Quarried limestone for building and landscaping

Butterfield Color
www.butterfieldcolor.com
800-282-3388
Concrete colorant, stains, stamps

The Colonial Stoneyard
www.thecolonialstoneyard.com
978-448-3329
*Natural stone and stone products
for landscaping*

Concrete Art
www.concreteart.net
800-500-9445
*Decorative scoring and staining
system*

Coverall Stone, Inc.
www.coverallstone.com
800-779-3234
*Natural stone columns, tiles,
pebbles, fountains, benches*

Cultured Stone
www.culturedstone.com
800-255-1727
Manufactured stone

**D. A. Spencer Natural Stone
Water Sculptures, Inc.**
www.naturalstonewater
sculptures.com
585-924-7542
Hand-carved stone sculptures

EP Henry Corporation
www.ephenry.com
800-444-3679
Concrete pavers, blocks, veneers

GardenMolds
www.gardenmolds.com
800-588-7930
*Steppingstone and edging
molds for concrete*

General Shale Brick
www.generalshale.com
800-414-4661
*Brick, concrete masonry, clay and
concrete pavers, wall systems*

Goshen Stone Co., Inc.
www.goshenstone.com
413-268-7171
Natural stone

High Plains Stone
www.highplainsstone.com
303-791-1862
*Building, masonry, and
landscaping stone*

**Hi-Tech Architectural
Products**
www.granitepaving.com
*Granite and concrete cobbles
and pavers*

The Home Depot
www.homedepot.com
*Building and landscaping
materials, patio furnishings*

**Keystone Retaining
Wall Systems**
www.keystonewalls.com
800-747-8971
Retaining wall systems

Lakeview Stone and Garden
www.lakeviewstone.com
206-525-5270
*Natural flagstone, wall stone,
cobble, river rock, and veneer*

Lang Stone Company
www.langstone.com
800-589-5264
*Full range of natural stone
products*

Little Meadows Stone Co.
www.littlemeadowsstone.com
866-305-3250
*Natural Pennsylvania landscape
stone*

Lowe's Home Improvement
www.lowes.com
*Building and landscaping
materials, patio furnishings*

**Lyngso Garden
Materials, Inc.**
www.lyngsogarden.com
650-364-1730
*Natural stone, construction
materials*

L & W Stone Corporation
www.lwstonecorp.com
800-346-9739
*Natural stone pavers, boulders,
veneer*

Manufacturer's Mineral Co.
425-228-2120
*Natural rock, concrete and
masonry*

Marenakos Rock Center
www.marenakos.com
425-392-3313
*Full-service stone yard
specializing in natural stone for
paths, walls, and water features*

Modello Designs
www.modelloconcrete.com
800-663-3860
*Concrete patterns and decorative
finishes*

Mutual Materials
www.mutualmaterials.com
800-477-3008
*Manufacturer and distributor of
masonry and hardscape products*

Oly-Ola Edgings
www.olyola.com
800-EDGINGS
Path edging products

Original Color Chips
www.originalcolorchips.com
800-227-8479
Concrete coatings and finishes

Pacific Stone Co., Inc.
www.pacificstoneco.com
888-722-7866
*Natural stone for patios, pathways,
and garden walls; concrete
paving stone, decorative step
stones, and block retaining walls*

Paver Search
www.paversearch.com
Paver products and resources

Robinson Brick
www.robinsonbrick.com
800-477-9002
Brick and thin true-stone veneer

SoCal Custom Concrete
www.socalcustomconcrete.com
714-265-7134
*Stamped concrete, coatings,
resurfacing, and other finishes*

Soil Retention Systems, Inc.
www.soilretention.com
800-346-7995
*Plantable and permeable
concrete wall and paving systems*

Sonoma Cast Stone
www.sonomastone.com
877-939-9929
Concrete tile and pavers

StoneDeck West, Inc.
www.stonedeckwest.com
877-686-4759
Natural stone decking systems

Sure-loc Edging
www.surelocedging.com
800-787-3562
*Aluminum and steel landscape
and paver edging*

The Stone Yard
www.stoneyard.com
800-231-2200
*Natural building and land-
scaping stone*

credits

Photographers

William Abranowicz/Art + Commerce: 38; Amateur Gardening/IPC+ Syndication: 61 top right, 93 bottom, 161 bottom center; **courtesy of Ames True Temper:** 84 top row #4, 84 bottom row center; **Brigid Arnott/acpsyndication.com/ JBG Photo:** 144 top; **Photoshot/ Red Cover/Steve Back:** 134; **Pernilla Bergdahl/Gap Photos:** 45 bottom; **Elke Borkowski/ Gap Photos:** 34, 54 top; **Brand X Pictures/Getty Images:** 85 bottom row #1; **Kira Brandt/ Living Inside:** 161 bottom right (styling: Gaia Rasmussen); **Marion Brenner:** front cover, 10, 11 top, 15 top, 23, 24 right, 27, 28 bottom, 32 top left, 32 bottom, 33, 43 bottom, 45 top, 50 top, 53 top right, 57 top, 57 bottom, 61 top left, 65 bottom, 75 bottom left, 96, 97 top left, 102, 103 top center, 103 top right, 104, 128, 139 bottom left, 147 bottom left, 148 top left, 148 bottom left, 148 bottom right, 162, 163 top #1, 163 top #2, 169 left, back cover bottom; **Marion Brenner/Getty Images:** 30; **Rob D. Brodman:** 103 bottom center, 159 bottom right (design: Roberta Walker Landscape Design); **Jason Busch/ acpsyndication.com/JBG Photo:** 93 top center, 136–137; **Van Chaplin:** 125 top left, 125 top center, 125 top right; **Jennifer Cheung:** 140 top left (design: Glen Brouwer, Integration Design Studio, in collaboration with Carmela and Miles Phillips); 141 (design: Brian Kissinger, Thomas and Todd); **Peter Christiansen:** 152 top #4; **Steve Cory:** 81 bottom, 109 bottom; **Jack Coyier:** 148 top right (design: Richard Krumwiede, Architerra Design Group); **Creative Crop/Getty Images:** 85 top row #1; **Sarah Cuttle/Gap Photos:** 168 left (design: Lesley Faux); **Daley + Gross:** 42–43; **Frederic Didillon/ Gap Photos:** 94; **Andrew Drake:** 125 bottom; **Frederic Ducout/**

Living Inside: 7; Photoshot/Red Cover/Ron Evans: 140 bottom right; Cheryl Fenton: 155 top #2; FhF Greenmedia/Gap Photos: 50 bottom (design: Claire Whitehouse); Scott Fitzgerrell: 84 top row #2, 84 top row #3; Roger Foley: 4–5, 6, 8, 17, 18–19, 20 top, 25, 26–27, 28 top, 35 top, 40 top right, 49 top, 56–57, 66, 86, (landscape design: Tom Mannion), 119 top right (design: Donna Hackman), 126, 138, 139 top right, 139 bottom right, 140 top right, 140 bottom left, 143 top right, 144 bottom left, 153, 154, 161 bottom left, 166, 167 left; Anne Fonnesbech/Living Inside: 36 bottom; Ashley Elizabeth Ford: 169 right (design: Ketti Kupper Art + Design); Thomas Fricke/Corbis: 147 top right; Frank Gaglione: 79 right, 81 top left, 81 top right, 83 left, 83 center, 84 bottom row left, 84 bottom row right, 85 middle row #1, 85 middle row #3, 85 bottom row #3, 85 bottom row #4, 87 top left, 87 top right, 87 bottom left, 89 all, 91 top left, 91 top right, 92 all, 93 top left, 107 top right, 109 top right, 113 top center, 113 top right, 116 all, 117 all, 127 top left, 127 top center, 127 top right, 133 all, 135 all, 152 top #3, 152 bottom #1, 152 bottom #2, 152 bottom #3, 155 top #1, 155 top #3, 155 top #4, 155 bottom right, 156 bottom #1, 156 bottom #2, 156 bottom #3; Gap Photos: 142, 143 left; Tria Giovan: 41; David Goldberg/Susan Roth & Co.: 156 top (design: Richard Wogisch); Art Gray: 110–111 (design: Peter Eberhard and Greg Sanchez, GDS Designs); Simon Griffiths/acpsyndication. com/JBG Photo: 19 top, 43 top, 114; Steven A. Gunther: 73 top right (design: Jeffrey Gordon Smith Landscape Architecture), 75 bottom right, 80 (design: Katherine Spitz), 106, 151 bottom (design: Michael Buccino, Michael Buccino Associates); Harpur Garden Library/Corbis: 40

bottom; Jerry Harpur/Gap Photos: 44 (design: Ossart and Mauriers), 54–55 (design: Topher Delaney), 39 top, 161 top right (design: Grover Dear); Marcus Harpur/Harpur Garden Images: 64 (design: Jamie Dunstan); Philip Harvey: 85 top row #2, 85 top row #3, 151 top #4; Photoshot/Red Cover/Ken Hayden: 37; Saxon Holt: 48–49, 119 top left, 157, back cover top; Maree Homer/acpsyndication.com/JBG Photo: 14–15, 63 top, back cover middle; D. A. Horschner/Design Workshop: 88 (design: Faith Okuma); iStockphoto.com: 85 top row #5, 85 top row #6, 85 top row #7; Bjarni B. Jacobsen/Pure Public/Living Inside: 13; Jon Jensen: 72 (landscape contractor: Dean DeSantis, DeSantis Landscapes), 74 (landscape contractor: Dean DeSantis, DeSantis Landscapes); Jetta Productions/Getty Images: 82; Simon Kenny/acpsyndication .com/JBG Photo: 22; Photoshot/Red Cover/Corinne Korda: 164 left; Chuck Kuhn: 103 top left, 103 bottom left, 103 bottom right, 107 top left, 107 middle left, 107 middle right, 107 bottom left, 107 bottom right, 112 all, 113 right inset, 121 top left, 121 top right, 123 top #1, 123 top #2, 123 top #3, 123 top #4, 123 bottom left, 123 bottom center, 151 top #1, 151 top #2, 151 top #3; Beau Lark/Photolibrary: 130; Jorgen Larsson/Nordicphotos/Corbis: 12; Fiona Lea/Gap Photos: 67; Holly Lepere: 149 (design: Alida Aldrich, the Aldrich Company); Chris Leschinsky: 1, 9, 21 (design: Jeffrey Gordon Smith Landscape Architecture; Kevin O'Donnell, Sequoia Pacific Landscape), 31, 36 top, 47, 51 (design: Jeffrey Gordon Smith Landscape Architecture; Kevin O'Donnell, Sequoia Pacific Landscape), 58–59, 62–63, 63 bottom, 65 top right (design Jeffrey Gordon Smith Landscape Architecture), 73 bottom, 97 top

right, 97 bottom, 113 top left, 119 bottom, 124, 159 bottom left, 167 center, 170, 172; Mark Luscombe-Whyte/IPC+ Syndication: 98–99; Allan Mandell: 109 top center; Jim McCausland: 78; Fiona McLeod/Garden Picture Library/Photolibrary: 20 bottom; Shelley Metcalf: 46 top, 58 top, 58 bottom; Clive Nichols/Gap Photos: 160 (design: Charlotte Rowe), 161 top center (design: Joe Swift Lighting: Garden and Security Lighting), 168 right (design: D Stevens and J. Dowle); Clive Nichols/Photo-library: 132; Brian North/Gap Photos: 53 bottom right (design: Rachel De Thame), 54 bottom (design: Hugo Bugg and Maren Hallenga); Photoshot/Red Cover/Martyn O'Kelly: 139 top left; courtesy of Oly-Ola Edgings Inc.: 91 bottom; Photoshot/Red Cover/Jerry Pavia: 19 bottom, 35 bottom, 65 top left, 174; Victoria Pearson/Getty Images: 122; Norm Plate: 70–71 (design: Diana Stratton, Diana Stratton Design), 76 (design: Scott Junge); courtesy of Portland Cement Association: 108 bottom left; Photoshot/Red Cover/Practical Pictures: 150; Howard Rice/Gap Photos: 163 top #4; courtesy of Robinson Brick: 155 bottom left; Susan A. Roth: 115 bottom (design: Landscapes by Atlantic); Mark Rutherford: 85 top row #4; Jeremy Samuelson/Getty Images: 165 left, 167 right; Loren Santow: 109 top left; Photoshot/Red Cover/Kim Sayer: 77 bottom; David Schiff: 84 top row #1, 85 middle row #4, 85 bottom row #2; Photoshot/Red Cover/Shania Shegedyn: 146; Jason Smalley/Gap Photos: 90; Gary Smith/Photolibrary: 93 top right; Stockbyte/Getty Images: 85 middle row #2; Thomas J. Story: 68–69, 118 (design: Kathleen Shaeffer), 159 top left; Friedrich Strauss/Gap Photos: 32 top right; Tim Street-Porter: 11 bottom, 15 bottom, 24 left, 46 bottom,

49 bottom, 144 bottom right, 147 bottom right, 158, 164 right; Tim Street-Porter/Beateworks/Corbis: 60; Tim Street-Porter/Corbis: 165 right; Dan Stultz: 83 right, 155 bottom center; Derek Swalwel/acpsyndication.com/JBG Photo: 163 top #3; Claire Takacs/Photolibrary: 100–101; Nicola Stocken Tomkins/25 Beautiful Gardens/IPC+ Syndication: 29, 61 bottom right; Nicola Stocken Tomkins/IPC+ Syndication: 147 top left; E. Spencer Toy: 156 bottom #4; Mark Turner: 120; John Paul Urizar/acpsyndication.com/JBG Photo: 161 top left; Dominique Vorillon: 39 bottom; Howard Walker/Amateur Gardening/IPC+ Syndication: 52–53; Darren Warner/IPC+ Syndication: 143 bottom right; Michael Wee/acpsyndication.com/JBG Photo: 16; Rob Whitworth/Gap Photos: 159 top right; Michele Lee Willson: 152 top #1, 152 top #2, 152 bottom #4; Michael Winokur: 108 bottom right; Tim Winter/Woman & Home/IPC+ Syndication: 145; Photoshot/Red Cover/Mark York: 40 top left

Illustrators

Bill Oetinger: 73 top left, 77 top right, 87 bottom right, 108 top, 111, 115 all, 123 bottom right, 129 all; Rik Olson: 75 top left, 127 bottom left, 127 bottom right; Damien Scogin: 77 top left, 79 all, 95 all, 99 all, 101 all, 105 all, 131 all

Special Thanks

Georgia Dodge, Mark Hawkins, Stephanie Johnson, Brianne McElhiney, Haley Minick, Kimberley Navabpour, Marie Pence, Alan Phinney, Lorraine Reno, Margaret Sloan, Vanessa Speckman, E. Spencer Toy

index